DOES GOD REALLY CARE?

Be amazed by a true story of God's outrageous blessings during difficult times of trials.

By: Bob and Gloria Bruce

xulon PRESS

Does God Really Care?
Be amazed by a true story of God's outrageous blessings during difficult times of trials.
by Bob and Gloria Bruce

Printed in the United States of America

ISBN 978-1-60477-912-7

www.xulonpress.com

ENDORSEMENTS

You will say, "God really does care!" after reading Bob's and Gloria's amazing account! Learn how God stayed with them as they faced life's most challenging times. For over 35 years my wife Carole and I have seen proof of Gods direct intervention in their lives. Be encouraged and know God really cares for you!

Larry Arendas, Pastor, President of Spirit and Truth Ministries International Terrell, North Carolina

Amazing story of God's faithfulness and the Bruces' too. It is such a treasure for those who read it and an encouragement to me.

Marion Moe, Author, Editor and Women's Bible Teacher, Christchurch, New Zealand

Bob and Gloria are inspirations to those going through crises and adversity. The world is full of people wondering where God is when the going gets tough. They have found God in the tough times.

George Hoyt, Connections Coordinator, Reynolda Presbyterian Church Winston Salem, North Carolina

I've heard Bob Bruce bless so many groups with his story that I'm thrilled it's finally in book form. Get ready for a blessing. You will never be the same after reading this powerful testimony!

Stu Epperson Jr. Nationally Syndicated Radio Host of Truth Talk Live

He truly gave the Bruces beauty for ashes!

Ann Miller, Coordinator for Reynolda Presbyterian Church's ministry for the Bruce's

No matter what circumstances the Bruces encountered, they always had a smile for everyone. Their joy is a continuous reminder of God's love for them—a real example for all of us—that God really does care.

Jan Rice, a sister in Christ, Reynolda Presbyterian Church

Bob and Gloria are an inspiration to all of us who face struggles in life. They taught us how to go through the fire with character and come out into a land of peace and prosperity. God continues to smile upon them.

Jeffrey L. Deaton, M.D. Winston Salem, N.C.

I believe the Bruces have truly captured the essence of God's reason for allowing trials in our lives. It has been an encouragement to me and makes me want to draw close to God knowing that one of His greatest gifts is His ability to turn even our most difficult trials into a blessing!

Bob Dunlap, President, Fidelis SecureCare, Inc. of North Carolina

It has been my great privilege to see the story of Job retold before my very eyes. I trust that the reader of this book will be similarly blessed. As I watched the Bruces walk by faith through one trial after another, my faith grew. Early on, Bob mentioned to me that he had asked God to give him a faith greater than a mustard seed. This book is a testimony to God's faithfulness in answering that prayer. Victory in Jesus, indeed!

Mickey Thigpen, Executive Director Reynolda Presbyterian Church

I have been privileged to look out from the platform in three countries and see the responses of hundreds and thousands to this incredible testimony of Bob Bruce. Now, to see this fully

written down brings to me hope that an even wider audience will have this Christian experience. And with the companion word of his beloved, incredibly mature, Gloria, this book should become well known in Christian circles and beyond. I commend this testimony of life for a number of reasons:

- It is perhaps one of the finest dealings with the problem of theodicy available today. Being altogether scriptural and of real life issues, it is reliable and fresh. Why is there suffering if God is good comes clear.
- This is the testimony of a thoroughly humble and self-effacing man. It took a clear word from the Lord to get him to write this down and have it published. There is no boasting here. It is about God's caring.
- The title "God really cares" permeates every page. Today's confusion over "the prosperity gospel" has obfuscated this basic word of God's care. Every trial described in this testimony is a "platform" of Christ revealing Himself as a caregiver.
- The local congregation rarely is seen as the place of miracles today. Bob Bruce's story is right there in his church, a wonderful Body of Christ, where he has been a layman leader for many years.
- It is addressed to you, the reader. With no wasted words, in current parlance, a mature voice is speaking, "Know today that God cares about your trials. Stop wrestling, and put your trust and your future in God."
- It deals with heart issues, suffering, losses of homes and jobs. The talk is tough-talk; about the Grace to endure and even prosper through times of trial. "Never give up" is totally understood to mean "Never give in to the temptations of despair, which are from the devil."
- It is not "God talk." Bob and Gloria are so Jesus-centered that they can make sense of "God is good all the time" kind of slogans. Their story is a present-day fulfillment of "Someday it will all make sense."

- Today's hassle over John 14:6, "I am the way, there is no other," is a commonplace argument within and outside the church of Christ. I can only say that in secular Bulgaria, South Africa, and in the U.S.A., I have seen thousands hear this testimony and weep, and many joyfully join in the Sinner's Prayer, as I have.

Hank Keating
President of Keating Christian Ministries, Inc.

ACKNOWLEDGEMENTS

There are a number of important people who helped bring this book into existence. First, I would like to thank New Canaan Society of Winston-Salem for the invitation for me to give my testimony before some 100 men. When I was finished one person came up to me and said, "You ought to write your story as a testimony book." Immediately it came to me "Yes." Although many people had said, "you should write a book" in the last five years, I had always dismissed the suggestion. This time, as I went home immediately ideas and thoughts starting coming. I asked Gloria to co-author the book.

We so appreciate the willingness of our two daughter-and-laws Amanda Bruce and Ellen Bruce, for their hours of help in clarifying thoughts, sentence structure and grammar. Christopher Bruce was a capable advisor and patient teacher of the workings of Microsoft Word. Mimi Williams who is a professional editor did the final superb editing job.

Finally, I would like to thank Pastor Alan Wright for writing the Forward and for those that wrote endorsements.

FORWARD

A woman presses through a chaotic mob, her heart throbbing with a mixture of desperation, fear and longing. Her seemingly interminable suffering has left her with this one hope – a rabbi from Galilee. When she touches him, she feels a warm glow of healing energy infuse her diseased body. She is terrified, but the Messiah smiles, "Your faith has healed you."

A man falls on his knees, his leprous face insensitive to the wetness of his own tears, as he begs, "If you are willing, you can make me clean." Jesus' touch is the first human contact the infected beggar has felt in years. "I am willing – be clean!" Like a bath of cool light, the Savior's healing virtue washes away the years of disease.

A hurricane sweeps along the shores of Crete with such violence that the panicky sailors chunk their provisions overboard, but one man on deck proclaims a strange assurance of survival. "Last night an angel of the God ... whom I serve ... said, 'Do not be afraid, Paul. You must stand trial before Caesar; and God has graciously given you the lives of all who sail with you." The ship, and everything in it, is swallowed by the pounding surf, but, just as the man of God had been told, no sailor dies that day.

As a preacher, I live amidst such miracle stories of the Bible.

As a pastor, I also live amidst the painful stories of hurting people.

And, everyday, I wait and watch for those two worlds to merge.

The story you are about to read is the most glorious such intersection I have ever known.

Some point to the apparent absence of any such miracle stories in their friends' lives as evidence that the miraculous ministry of Jesus has expired. When all the theological debate calms, they look at you and say, "Well, do you know any miracle stories like those in the Bible?" Too often, we find ourselves telling about a condition that might have been healed without supernatural help, admitting that we can't say for sure. Or, so often we find ourselves pointing to a poorly documented story of an unusual miracle in a remote land.

Conversely, some speak so casually of their recurrent miracle stories that it beggars my belief. I just don't think that God gives us visions every time we brush our teeth or that God rushes in and heals us every time we sneeze. I am left wondering if some saints' much ado about God's lavish interventions is an elaborate form of denial. When we tell our miracle stories without telling our suffering stories, we're all left feeling disconnected because we know that in this world we will all face trouble.

The story you are about to read is miraculous. It is the story of non-functional internal organs and glands being re-activated like the broken uterus of that bleeding woman. It is the story of incurable skin disorders and boils being washed away like that of the leprous beggar. It is the story of how a cataclysmic catastrophe can devour everything a man owns but never touch the man or his family.

But, be assured, the story you are about to read is not glibly told. It does not rush past the pain to its happy ending. Why does it not? Because it is a real story. It is not a story about a mythical native in an obscure jungle. It is about a real man, Bob Bruce, and his family. He's been my friend, my parishioner, and my partner in ministry for a decade. I know him intimately. I love him deeply. I remember the joy of meeting him for the first time. I remember his body when it was ravaged by cancer. I remember his raw, irradiated neck. I remember meeting after meeting with him as he sipped on an ever present water bottle since there was no saliva. I remember his granddaughter in the hospital. I remember his house in ashes. I watched him pray. I watched him hurt. I watched him believe. I watched him persevere. This is a story about a real man. I write in part to bear witness to the veracity of this testimony. Whatever shreds of credibility have accumulated in my 20 years of pastoral ministry I hereby place on the line to assure you that everything you are about to read is true.

In the midst of life's desperate times, we wonder if God still works miracles.

He does.

In real life, we face trouble and sometimes, and, as we wait on God for much longer than seems reasonable, we wonder if God really cares.

He does.

And while we wait, we sometimes wonder if God has a plan for us.

He does.

He did for Bob and Gloria. He does for you too.

Alan Wright
Sr. Pastor, Reynolda Presbyterian Church
Author of *A Childlike Heart, Lover of My Soul,*
God Moments and *Shame Off You*

CONTENTS

* Written by Gloria. All other chapters written by Bob

TO GOD BE THE GLORY

This book is dedicated to the glory of God.

The purpose of this testimony is to draw your attention to the miracles we experienced. Our circumstances are not important, but they must be stated so you can understand the mighty works of our God in our lives.

> "One generation shall praise your works to another and shall declare Your mighty acts, on the glorious splendor of your majesty, and on your wonderful works, I will meditate. Men shall speak of the power of your awesome acts and I tell of your Greatness. They shall eagerly utter the memory of Your abundant goodness and will shout joyfully of thy righteousness."
>
> Psalm 145:4-7

> "Lest you forget the things which your eyes have seen, and lest they depart from your heart all the days of your life; but make them known to your sons and your grandsons."
>
> Deuteronomy 4:9

The following is a true story of God's involvement in our lives, during a very difficult time in the Robert C. Bruce family. This book is the spiritual legacy to our six children, their spouses, our 13 grandchildren, and to our future grandchildren.

EARLY YEARS

Thankfully, I was born into a blessed Christian family. Certainly more blessed than I could understand or imagine. My father had a good stable job in a steel company rising in the ranks of management. My mother was a stay-at-home mother and wife. Dad was a Presbyterian and mother a devote Catholic. In those days, the non-Catholic had to agree to bring the children up in the Catholic Church. I navigated my way through elementary school, high school and college, all run by the Catholic Church. As a young Catholic boy at age ten I assisted the priest at Mass as an altar boy. The Mass was spoken in Latin. I remember the long hours I spent learning the Latin responses. Finally, I passed the required test and was so excited to put on the black cassock and white surplice over the cassock. They always broke the new kids in during the summer. Because they also had trouble getting boys to assist the priest early in the morning, I served Mass five days a week mostly at 7:00 A.M. Although I didn't understand the Mass, I was thrilled.

One day, for reasons I can't explain, I stayed after Mass and after the lights were turned out. The priest departed from the altar but the incense was thick and still floating in the air as I knelt at the altar. While kneeling there, a strange feeling came over me. It was like a peace, but much more, a little like a presence, maybe a glow. I was captivated by it. I had no idea what it was, but I knew from that very first encounter I would stay after Mass again the next day. That feeling stayed with me as long as I knelt there. After about ten minutes, being a young boy and fasting until after the Mass, I would begin feeling rumblings in my stomach and decide it was time to go home for breakfast. When I got up and left the altar the presence would leave. So, I went about my day as any other normal ten-year-old. The next morning exactly the same happening occurred. What I began to do during these times was to talk to Jesus conversationally. I hadn't memorized any English prayers so I couldn't pray formal prayers. All I could do is begin telling Jesus about my day. This went on all summer. Eventually my prayers changed; I wanted to praise Jesus and worship Him in the silent church with just the two of us there. It was during that summer that I invited Jesus into my heart. Although at the time, I was clueless as to what that meant. I had never heard the term "born again," but God knew my heart and He came and the Holy Spirit took up residence in me. It was such a wonderful time. It was over half a century ago, but I can still smell that incense and vividly remember it just as if it were yesterday.

I thought I was alone in that church. Not so. Lurking behind the pillars were the priests watching this strange kid. They began to take an interest in me. They invited me to dinners and even took me to a couple monasteries for overnight visits. They thought they had caught a fish for a future seminary student and eventually a priest. This went on for a number of years. In the end, I did not choose to enter the seminary. My younger brother Terry did. At age 14, Terry entered the seminary. He studied for ten years, was ordained, and has been a priest for over 40 years. For me, the strange presence ceased, along with my altar boys days, and I forgot about the experience.

After college, I took a turn away from the things of God and began pursuing materialistic things. I was ambitious, wanting to make a name for myself. I believed I could be self-sufficient, independent and didn't need God in my life except on Sunday morning and for emergencies or big events. I was seeking first the kingdom of Bob Bruce, and hoping all the good things in life would come to me through hard work.

I began to earnestly look for a wife. I had been praying for God to give me one for about 10 years before I met Gloria Gausselin. I learned that TWA had a training school that housed the flight attendant students in one large motel. My best friend Bob and I called to ask for two partners for a game of bridge. Gloria and her friend Rory answered the request and we four started playing bridge regularly, as well as going to movies, dinners etc. One day my friend Bob told me he had asked Gloria to marry him. He said he was one of several who had proposed to her; in fact she was engaged to another guy attending Michigan State.

Bob graduated from college and returned home, planning to come back the next weekend and stay at my house so he could see Gloria. On Wednesday night, Gloria asked me if I would go with her to look at a car for sale. On the way home we stopped at a dance hall and had a great time. She called Bob the next day and told him not to come visit and two days later on Friday we had our official first date. We had spent four months together already but as a foursome. I was always dating women Gloria fixed me up with while she was dating my friend Bob. Imagine my shock when Gloria asked me to marry her, on that first date! My reply was, "you are already engaged to someone else," and she said, "I could fix that." We were officially engaged three months later, and Gloria and I were married in 1963. God really answered my prayer for a good wife in a surprising way. Gloria was surely His choice and mine, as we have been married for forty-five years and blessed with six children.

Nine months and one day after our wedding our daughter Sherri was born, and two years later her brother Robert was born. As the kids got into school we began to realize they needed spiritual teachings. That began a quest to seek a spiritual base. We had never stopped going to weekly Mass, yet it seemed like a formal obligation rather than a growing personal relationship. Deep inside I wasn't happy with the smoking, drinking and the direction of my life. I was searching for something but didn't know what it was. In 1970 at the age of 30 I found what I was looking for. I found it under some unusual circumstances at a Faith at Work Conference in the Pocono Mountains. In fact, Gloria had the same experience at the same conference. It was there that our whole life was turned around when we had an encounter with the Holy Spirit. Guess what one of the first phenomenon I experienced again was? You guessed it... the Divine Presence. Except now that unknown feeling had a name it was the Holy Spirit.

The encounter changed the compass of our lives. We became involved in Holy Spirit renewal in both the Catholic and Protestant churches. Over a period of time, the Holy Spirit involved us increasingly with the Protestant movement of God. I explained to my Catholic friends that God was moving us into the northern part of the vineyard; whereas, they were working the same spiritual vineyard except in the southern vineyard. We were all working for the same Vine Master to the best of our abilities. Now 39 years later, I am very thankful for these early beginnings in the Catholic Church but God has never led us back to the southern vineyard, although there is plenty of fruit to be harvested in both vineyards. Now those early years seem a distant past, but that Divine Presence is as fresh as it was when I was a ten-year-old boy kneeling at the altar.

We continued to grow in grace and the knowledge of the Lord. We also continued to add to the family. Scott was born in Bethlehem, Pennsylvania in 1971, followed by Christopher in 1973. David was born in Boston, Massachusetts in 1975. Lastly came Terry born in 1982. In 1985, we moved to Claremont, California with all 5 boys. Sherri was engaged and therefore remained in Boston.

TELL THE GREAT DEEDS GOD HAS DONE

Life has its twists and turns! It was a typical sunny day in Los Angeles in May 1997 when my boss called me into his office on the 27th floor of a high rise in downtown Los Angeles. I expected it to be the usual budget meeting. Instead, after five years of working for a major bank, my boss said I was being downsized. This was not the first time I experienced this, but it was the first time at age 59, not a good age to look for another corporate job. I had no other option but to begin a job search. Three months later, after countless resumes had been sent out, a headhunter called with an opportunity in North Carolina with a major bank named Wachovia. The actual hiring process took about two months.

We were sad at the prospect of leaving California and three of our sons. Our son Scott married Amanda White in November 1997. Amanda was Scott's high school sweetheart and this was a long awaited event. We did not know for certain at the wedding that we would be leaving. We look back on the uncertainty as God's mercy. We were able to rejoice at the wedding rather than focus on moving and leaving three sons and a new daughter-in-law behind. Having had six months of unemployment I spent time helping Scott find a house, fix it and paint it. The actual job offer came the week following the wedding.

It was extraordinary for a major organization to be interested in hiring someone my age. They not only gave me a generous offer including a signing bonus, good salary, and full fringe benefit package but they also paid for all the relocation costs. So, we moved to what we considered a new part of the country, Winston-Salem, North Carolina. I started a new chapter in my book of life with my wife Gloria, and Terry, our youngest son.

Life was good for 13 months, until I was once again called into the office of my boss. He informed me the bank was going through a major merger. Our department, Human Resources, was the first to be downsized. This began the most incredible four years of my life. I had moved Terry at age 15 across the country from southern California to North Carolina. To move a teenager in the middle of his sophomore year is not good timing. We were amazed and blessed at how well he had transitioned and he said he loved North Carolina. I told Terry that although I no longer had a job with Wachovia we would not move again until after he graduated from high school. The only problem was that I still needed to work. Now looking for a job in my sixties in a downsized labor market was going to be even a bigger a challenge. We did not really expect to find a job in the Winston-Salem area; but we were willing to use our financial resources to remain there for Terry's sake.

I had begun to get some job leads when one day while driving home from Virginia I heard the Lord clearly whisper into my thoughts, "You are finished working for the secular world, from now on you are on My payroll." We had checked our finances and calculated we could survive until Terry graduated from high school, but permanently? I was still two years away from Social Security. This would take a huge leap of faith. Yet after praying and asking for peace from God, Gloria and I were sure it was the Lord. I immediately stopped looking for a job. Incredibly, now eight years later I am amazed at how He provides income in the most unusual ways. Our income has continued to equal the paycheck that I received my last year at the bank! He is so faithful.

One day while reading, I looked up at the ceiling in thought and discovered two pea-sized lumps in my jaw. They weren't visible unless I stretched my neck and then they would pop out. They weren't sore but after giving them ample time to go away, I decided to have them checked out. I had three biopsies and all three came back benign. With a big sigh of relief, we proceeded with our plans for a trip to Germany to visit with two of our sons who were both working in Europe.

It seemed crazy in a way, to take this trip considering our financial position. However, Terry was a senior in high school and when would such an opportunity come along again? Christopher was spending the year playing professional basketball and coaching in Esbjerg, Denmark. David had graduated from Point Loma University in May and took a job with the Armed Forces Recreation Center (AFRC) in Garmisch, Germany. The AFRC ran two hotels' catering to members of the Armed Forces on leave for R&R with their families. Terry, Chris, Gloria and I arrived in Munich at the same time, rented a car and drove south to join David. David worked nights at the resort and spent the days snowboarding the majestic Alps. It was in the heart of Bavaria and very picturesque. We were visiting during the Christmas holiday break and against that idyllic backdrop we ushered in the 21st Century. We had one of the most blessed, anointed, fun times in our lives. It was a winter wonderland the last week in December 1999 in Germany. It is surely a trip that stands out in our minds as something special. We are so glad that we did not know what was lurking around the corner. Such knowledge would have canceled the trip.

Before we left for Germany, my doctor informed me that the benign lumps should be removed. So, surgery was scheduled for the week we returned. After the operation, the surgeon met Gloria in the waiting room and said he was certain it was cancer. Tests were performed to confirm his diagnosis. In a subsequent meeting, he said I had a very rare, aggressive, fast growing cancer in which there were only 31 reported cases in the world! It was cancer of the salivary glands. News like this really rocks your world, but I didn't have much time to consider the difficulties as another surgery was scheduled the following week.

When I got the nasty "C" word the first feeling that came visiting was fear. I tried to hold it at bay, but it was lurking around the corner and poking me with its insidious long fingers. Cancer is scary; so frightening. The news hits you like a bolt of lightning. It strikes and leaves you shaken. New fears immediately surface. Cancer is tough, not only on you but also on all those who love you. We did the only thing we could do in the circumstances and that was to pray. We immediately went into prayer. Intense prayer went forth. Word went out through the Internet to our contacts around the world. People, churches, small groups were praying. Some not just once but ongoing praying over months. We would not let negative words or negative prayers or discouraging words come into our house.

Gloria and I both had previously experienced miraculous healing from medical situations in the past. I was healed the night before I was scheduled for another surgery in 1972. Gloria was healed from arthritis while sitting among 7000 people at a conference. We have prayed and seen results of so many other people being healed, so with confidence we prayed earnestly. Because of my need I reached out to God with greater fervency than ever before in prayer.

We know what the Bible says about healing. We have prayed and quoted God's Words many times.

> ➤ Psalm 103:2-3   Bless the Lord O my soul,… who heals all Your diseases
> ➤ Psalm 107:20   He sent His word and healed them
> ➤ Isaiah 53:5   By His scourging we are healed
> ➤ Proverbs 4:22   [Your words] are life to those that find them, and health to all their whole body

However, in my case, this time, miraculous healing or deliverance from the scalpel was not to be. This was not God's plan for me. He had a different plan that I would soon experience.

Before I went under the knife, I had two significant dreams. The first was a scene where I was on the operating table. My doctor was facing me in his blue scrubs. In flowing robes Jesus walks up behind the surgeon and put His arms around the surgeon, melding His forearms and hands into the forearms and hands of the surgeon. This dream gave me great comfort.

The second dream was a World War II scene. I was leading a patrol up the hill to capture the hill. I was wounded and taken down behind the line by the medics. I was wounded but not unto death.

A third encouragement came from my friend, Larry Arendas. I greatly respect his ability to hear from God. While in prayer Larry asked God if this was the time for Bob to dance around His throne. Larry heard the Father say, "I would love to have Bob Bruce dance around My throne but "NOT YET." I am living on "NOT YET" time. There is still more for me to do down here before I can dance around His throne for eternity up there. These were very personal words of encouragement from God to me.

In diligently seeking God's Word from the Bible God gave me three Scriptures that became cornerstone scriptures for what was about to come:

"I cried to Thee for help, and thou didst heal me...Thou has kept me alive."

Psalm 30:3

"My prayer is to You O Lord, at an acceptable time (in the fullness of time), (emphasis added) O God in the greatness of your loving kindness answer me."

Psalm 69.13

"Simon, Simon, behold, Satan has demanded permission to sift you like wheat; but I have prayed for you, that your faith may not fail; and you, when you have been restored strengthen your brothers."

Luke 22:31-32

I knew these scriptures were for me even if I had trouble understanding the relevance of the verse in Luke. I requested the Lord to give me an increased mustard seed of faith. According to book of Matthew, each of us is given a mustard seed. I asked the Father to give me an enlarged mustard seed and He did!

It also says in the book of Matthew "Do not be anxious for your life."[1] Well that is easier said than done, but Gloria and I were very much at peace going into the surgery. We believed God through His words in the Bible and the dreams he gave me.

So we did what we believed the Bible encouraged us to do. "Having done everything to stand, stand firm."[2] I set my focus on the surgery ahead of me.

Before the operation, the surgeon told me he would ruin my golf game by severing nerves in my neck and shoulder. I told him he couldn't ruin my golf game because I didn't have one. I have never once played golf. However, I did play a lot of tennis. My surgeon did proceed to ruin any chance of me playing tennis again.

I had to suffer through four operations. My arm was so punctured that they put a port under the skin so they could access the port rather than trying to find one of my collapsed blood veins. Before the first surgery, I told the team of doctors and nurses that many people were praying for them. It seemed to comfort them. I remember during the surgical preparation, while the staff was scurrying around, feeling an overwhelming peace and presence of the Lord flood over me. It was like nothing I had ever experienced before. I hoped they would take their sweet time because I was not in any hurry to be sedated. When they did begin, they filleted my neck and put it on my shoulder. They proceeded to remove 80% of my saliva glands, eight lymph nodes, muscle, and two cancerous tumors. The surgeon aggressively went after the cancer. Upon completion of the three-hour operation, he was convinced the surgery was a success and that he had removed all of the cancer. However, since there was not very much information on this type of cancer he strongly urged radiation.

I followed the doctors' advice and saw a radiologist. The radiologist said she was going to put my body under the maximum stress a human being could take. She also said to try to eliminate any other stress in my life. That is not easy to do, as I was unemployed, at age 61, facing college tuition for my 17-year-old son, and major medical bills.

I went through radiation requiring 35 treatments at a very high dosage five days a week for seven weeks. They were experimenting with a new drug in an attempt to minimize side effects. This treatment required me to sit with a tube in my arm for four hours immediately prior to radiation. After this treatment, I had to hurry and drive a block away to the radiation equipment. I had to make sure that the radiation began within ten minutes from the time of the tube withdrawal. The radiation was like having my teeth x-rayed. There was absolutely no pain just a short buzz. The only difference was they made me a facemask to go over my face and then screwed it down to the table. It held my head absolutely immobile and had marks on it to where to point the radiation machine. I remember going through half the treatments with no side effects. I thought, "This is going to be a breeze." Little did I realize the effects were cumulative and by the time it was over I was a very, very sick lad. The surgery to remove the cancer was easy compared to this.

They set the radiation so high that when they radiated me from the front it blistered my back. It reduced my cervical esophagus to the size of the end of a Cross ballpoint pen. It normally is about the size of a normal garden hose. As a result of the radiation I could not eat any solid food for a long, long time, 434 days to be exact! That was a long fast! In addition to no food, I also could not have liquids of any kind, which included water, coffee or ice chips. It was 300 days before I could start liquids. About 400 days into the ordeal, it took 50 painful minutes to eat a small cup of chocolate pudding. Eating was just not worth the pain. When trying to swallow anything it was like having a razor blade in the back of my mouth. I was kept alive by a tube directly into my stomach and nourished by an 8-ounce can of prescription food, like a Boost drink. I poured 4-6 cans a day through the tube. Now when I go to the beach, I am the only one with two navels! Once I could drink water, I had to carry a water bottle with me everywhere. If all of this wasn't bad enough, I lost my appetite and my taste buds. In addition, I developed a nasty case of 21 canker sores in my mouth (all at one time), ulcers on my shrunken esophagus, an incurable skin disease called Rosacea and a very bad yeast infection called Candida.

Through it all, I learned the importance of saliva in digestion and the preservation of teeth. Without saliva you develop dry mouth. It is what I used to call "cotton mouth," like the dry mouth you experience after a long race. Lying down further complicated this. My nose would clog up so I would have to breathe through my mouth, but this made the problem worse. For two and half years I was not able to sleep lying down. I slept sitting up all night in a chair. Not a good way to get a good night's sleep.

On a lighter note, I guess one good aspect of this was that I lost 50 pounds. I have tried to recruit others to my weight loss program. I emphasize the benefits of my weight loss program: easy to prepare meals, fast food, no clean up, and inexpensive when eating out. You can weigh any weight you want by pouring in fewer cans. If you want to weigh more, use more cans. I guess I am not an effective salesman as I have not been able to convert one person to my weight lost program.

After about 400 days the feeding tube developed problems. The doctor installed a new one and said it was amazing the first one had lasted so long. The following week, I was back again with the same problem and a third tube was installed; it too would not work. The fact that there didn't seem to be a solution scared me. If I couldn't use the tube or eat normally, how could I survive? I forced myself to start drinking the prescription formula regardless of the pain. I had no choice. So I forced four to six cans a day of vanilla… "Uggh!" I thought this was about the worst experience I could face. Little did I know what was ahead of us.

OUR FAMILY GROWS (Gloria)

Christopher called from Esbjerg, Denmark to say he decided to turn down the offer to renew his basketball contract. He had been playing professional basketball and teaching three basketball teams. He had left a great job in California to pursue his dream to live abroad, play basketball and coach. Chris said that the Lord spoke to him about not returning to California. Instead, he was to come to North Carolina to live with us, to help take care of his father and be there for support. Were we agreeable? We were thrilled!

Chris arrived at the end of May, just after Bob had completed his radiation treatments. He took over all the yard work and other chores that Bob couldn't do. Soon after arriving, Chris told me how hard it was to return home after four years of college, three years of employment and one year coaching. He was particularly anxious because he did not want me to try to help him find a mate. He said, "If you ever, even just point out a girl I will not ask her for a date." After repeating this lectures two or three more times, he seemed satisfied that I understood. Now all I could do was pray and ask the Lord for His help. Surely, I reasoned, if Chris found a wife, it was more likely that he would not return to his beloved California and surfing. We were truly delighted to have him around as a regular part of our lives again. Chris definitely needed a lot of help finding the perfect girl. He had showed me his list of ten points he wanted in a wife and I was sure no such girl existed.

In December, Chris flew on a Friday to Manhattan for the weekend to visit a college friend. A pretty girl caught his eye on the flight up to New York. Sunday night while reading the departure board, he saw the posted two-hour delay. He noticed the same pretty girl standing next to him and began a conversation. Two hours later, after talking non-stop with each other, Chris tried to change his seat to sit next to Jennifer Dunlap but the airline said the flight was full. After they sat down, someone in Jen's row asked Chris if he would mind moving so he could set next to his wife. The Lord arranged that detail by placing the wife in Chris's row. Chris was delighted to have more time to get to know Jen and silently thanked the Lord for His intervention. Jen had recently moved home and was living with her parents to lower her expenses while she paid off her graduate school loans. Jen's parents Annie and Bob Dunlap lived at Lake Norman about one hour from our home. At midnight, Chris rushed up the stairs to tell me, "Mom, I think I've just met the girl I am going to marry!" She was his age and Chris had already determined she passed his ten-point list. I knew this had to be God because no such girl could easily be found. In the book of Proverbs it says a "House and wealth are from fathers, but a prudent wife is from the Lord."[1] One and a half years later, Chris married Jen on the lawn at her parent's lakefront home. We all knew that the Lord had rewarded Chris's obedience and sacrifice to leave coaching and move to North Carolina to serve his father with the wife of his dreams.

In June of 2000, the rest of our family arrived for a week in a big house at Sunset Beach on the North Carolina coast. Scott and Amanda did not come as they were expecting their first child in August. In all, there were 13 of us. This was a blessing to have so many of us together for a week, but it was also difficult time for Bob. He was definitely not well enough for such an adventure. We were naïve and believed the doctor when she said three weeks following completion of radiation he would be okay. We waited an extra week for good measure, but it was exhausting for him. When we returned home to Winston-Salem with almost everyone gone, we were relieved it was over. We still had our oldest two grandchildren Amanda, 12 and Scott, 10 for another week. Then, Chris, Bob and I drove them home to Marlboro, Massachusetts. We called Sherri an hour before we got to her house to give her an update. She said, "Have you talked to Robert? You'd better call him." So, calling from a Massachusetts toll road rest stop, we learned the shocking news. Robert wanted to return home with his three-year-old twin girls Michelle and Danielle, and ten-month-old Bobby. Their mother had been out of rehab for a month but had returned to drugs. It was time for him to leave. He needed help taking care of the children. He had already faxed out four resumes and received a job offer to start August 1. The craziness of the beach had not ended; it had just begun. I was to be an acting mother of three little ones again at age 59. Suddenly, having Chris there was even more of a blessing, as chasing kids was for the young and able. Now in addition to the stress of cancer, we had the stress of a growing household. In May we were a family of three, and by August there were eight of us.

The Bible says, "Children are a gift from the Lord,"[2] and "blessed is the man whose quiver is full."[3] Many times when the Lord wants to bless you, He does it by blessing your children, as He did with the provision of Jen for Chris.

David had returned to California after the beach vacation to get a temporary job. He planned to go on a mission trip with Youth With A Mission (YWAM) based in Kona, Hawaii. He would have three months of discipleship training while in Hawaii and then two months in the Philippines. Before David left North Carolina, he told us he did not plan to marry until he was 33. At the time, David was 24. Five months after that declaration David called to say he had met Natalie Moe. She was at YWAM in Kona attending the School of Worship. She had grown up in New Zealand, and at age 17 moved to Atlanta to become a model. She had already completed a mission trip with YWAM and had traveled to China on an outreach. She had started a chapter of Models For Christ in Atlanta and at age 19 wrote a book for young girls called *Ignite the Fire*. They were engaged in December and we were thrilled for David. They seemed to have one heart and vision to minister to youth and were certain God was calling them to a life together. Six years have passed since their wedding. They formed a band called Luminous and have ministered to youth around the world. They have a two-year-old named Kaden who travels with them. He has already been to 17 countries. They have produced and recorded three CDs, and have been able to increase the reach of their ministry to young people through their band's website online (www.Luminousrock.com).

In spite of the trials we were going through, the Lord brought us much joy through hearing our prayers for our children and blessing them beyond what we could imagine.

NEW CRISES (Gloria)

Wow the house was full! When we searched to buy this house in 1998 it was with much prayer and asking God to direct us to the house He wanted for us. This was not a new experience for us because we had prayed the same prayers in 1974 in Boston, and again in 1985 in California. Each time we knew that God had indeed answered those prayers and had directed our steps to the house He chose for us. There were many confirmations afterward, to assure us we heard His voice and that the houses and locations were perfect for many reasons. In making the decision to buy the house in Winston-Salem, we were confident that the Lord was directing us as He did before, but we did not know why He had directed us to a house with six bedrooms. We had planned to downsize. After all there were only three of us. Yet we were quite sure we picked the right house. I commented to Bob after the offer was accepted, "I wonder what God has in mind for us with this much house?"

Now we knew why the Lord had chosen this house for our needs. Robert moved his family into the downstairs level. He took Terry's room and the three children went into the other bedroom. Chris had already moved into the guest room upstairs. That left my sewing room and the office, which also had an extra bed. Terry took the office room because he was going to be away most of the time at college.

I began a new workload of shopping, cooking, laundry and childcare. The twins were enrolled in a day care because I did not have the energy to care for three children full time. We did keep

Bobby at home with us and there were many blessings along with the work. Having a baby around was a great joy. The endless amount of tasks kept us busy and not focused on the trials Bob was continually facing.

It was October when we took the three children to the Dixie Classic Fair, as Robert had to work every other Saturday. We looked for diversions or events to help occupy them and us. Danielle became very weak and feverish at the fair so we cut our day short. The next day, the doctor said she had Guillain-Barre Syndrome (GBS) and sent her to Baptist Hospital. We learned it was an inflammatory disorder of the peripheral nerves. GBS is not hereditary or contagious and what causes it is unknown. GBS is characterized by numbness and weakness in the arms or legs and possible loss of movement in the legs, arms, upper body and face. Danielle experienced all of those symptoms and remained in Baptist Hospital for three weeks. A feeding tube was inserted in her nose. Danielle and Grandpa were now both fed by tubes. Our days were spent visiting Danielle and pulling her around the hospital in a wagon. She loved to ride the elevators. Besides the wagon to pull, we had to push Bobby in the stroller. On the weekends, Michelle was a part of the scene while we visited the great playrooms provided in Brenner Children's Hospital. The doctors and staff were wonderful and a great comfort as we waited for the disease to run its course.

When Danielle was well enough she was transferred to Amos Cottage, a children's rehab facility. She had to relearn to walk and to use her limbs, as well as to eat again. It was a slow process. She had daily scheduled therapies. Eventually, the feeding tube came out. Now the highlight of our visits involved pushing her wheelchair to the vending machine to buy Lay's potato chips. In December, the children at Amos did a Christmas performance. The girls were all dressed in red satin robes while they sang or danced. Danielle was not a dancer but she looked beautiful in her wheelchair while we cried and clapped for her courage. Danielle was allowed to come home on Christmas day for a visit. We were all up waiting for her. All of our children and their families flew in for the holidays and there were 17 of us. She arrived at 8:30 A.M. and announced "Merry Christmas everyone." It was a wonderful and special day, to once again rejoice being together. It was so hard to take her back to Amos Cottage. She cried all the way there. She was in Amos Cottage a total of eight weeks. The week after Christmas, she was allowed to come home. Pastor Hank Keating, who was on staff at Reynolda Presbyterian Church where we worship, had visited Danielle every day to pray for her. The prayers and support of Hank and so many others made the burden seem lighter.

THE FALL

One cold winter day on December 20, 2001, while getting two-year-old Bobby out of the car he grabbed my new glasses. I struggled to protect the glasses and my feeding tube as I was backing out of the back seat of the car. The door didn't shut entirely. So with my left foot, I tapped it shut, while holding Bobby off to my right side. I began to lose my balance and fell step by step to my right about eight feet. I realized I would crush Bobby by falling on him. So I held him up out of harm's way as I fell hitting the cold concrete full force with nothing to break my fall. I knew I was in trouble. Gloria came running and offered to call 911. I said, "Wait a minute. Let's see if I recover." I tried to get up by moving my leg and passed out for a brief moment then said, "O.K. now you can call 911." As I laid on the cold cement, I began to go into shock. Gloria brought me several quilts and soon the ambulance came, and I had a very uncomfortable ride to the hospital.

X-rays revealed a fractured hip. An emergency operation was scheduled that same night with a doctor who had already done three hip operations that day. I received a spinal injection so I didn't feel any pain. In addition I must have had a form of laughing gas. I didn't even know they were doing anything until I heard the hammer working. The operation was painless, but I could not say the same for that night or for the recovery. The doctor prescribed a morphine pump and encouraged me to use it freely. I used it frequently as the pain was terrible. I smashed that button 35 times through the night only to learn in the morning the pump hadn't been working. I couldn't believe that the very next morning they took me to physical therapy to exercise my fancy new eight-inch plate inserted into my hip. I was not very cooperative. I tried my best to sweet talk the young little physical therapist to back off and give me some mercy; she didn't listen at all.

The real problem began immediately after the insertion of the plate into my hip. It caused a major pain in my sciatic nerve. This produced a pain that not even the strongest narcotic pain pill, oxycontin, could alleviate. There were times early on when the pain from my nerve was so bad all I could do was focus on how to get rid of it. All other activities and thoughts disappeared. Pain is a cruel taskmaster. The pain was always there when I sat, or lay down. I took prescription sleeping pills to get through the night. The only time there was relief was when I was standing or walking; however, I couldn't stand or walk 24 hours a day.

To this day my hip troubles me but not the serious pain as in those early months and years. But at times, while driving a car or on airplanes it gets inflamed and painful. I have looked into having a hip replacement. Due to the eight-inch plate in my hip area the MRI shows black and therefore is not helpful. They can't tell if the hip needs replacement or if there are bone fragments floating in the area. I continue to seek other answers for relief from the pain.

Because I didn't have medical insurance, I told the doctor I wanted to go home for Christmas, which was in a few days. He said that would be okay. The night before I was to come home, I received a big blessing. Hank Keating came to my room and told me I would not have to pay for any expenses associated with the accident. I asked, "Why?" and Hank told me that Mickey Thigpin had contacted some friends at Reynolda Presbyterian Church where we attended and they said they would cover the expenses. The next day, I learned that Mickey had sent out 100 e-mails to the men's support group and funds began to flow in. I was so overwhelmed and touched by the Lord's kindness and blessed by His people's outrageous generosity. The medical bills were slow coming in during the time donations were being collected. The hospital bill came to over $17,642. The amount contributed, by over 100 people through Reynolda was $18,572. It was more than enough to cover all of the expenses.

The cancer and the fractured hip, the sciatic nerve problem, GBS with my granddaughter, and my son moving in with three little ones during my lowest time of recovery, put a strain on our lives. Did God really care? We thought surely that was the end of our trials. Or so we thought. Little did we know what was coming next!

FIRE!! GET OUT!! (Gloria)

B ob had been home from the hospital for one week following the surgery to repair his fractured hip. Jen and her mother Annie Dunlap were in town, and I met them at the mall to see the china and silverware choices Chris and Jen had picked out for their upcoming marriage. In hindsight I remember entering the car in the parking lot at the mall and smelling gasoline. I remembered Bob telling me to get gas. I decided it was too busy with shoppers to go to Sam's Club and I drove home. That decision may have saved my life. I pulled into the garage, which was under the kitchen and dining room of the house. I gathered my purse and keys and opened the car door and a loud explosion occurred. The cause of the explosion was a faulty fuel injector. As long as the car had been in the open air there was no danger. In the garage, however, the fumes combusted with the hot engine and immediately ignited. Halfway out of the car, I saw flames leaping from the engine. My first thought was "Oh no, I have to get the car out of the garage." My second thought was "too late for that," and I hurried to the back of the car to discover a trail of flames, about one and a half inches wide and 18 inches high from the trunk area shooting down the driveway to the street. I jumped as high as I could hoping to clear the flames and ran up the stairs to the kitchen. There was Bob, wearing his pajamas, using his walker, and looking at the hanging lamp now lying on the floor. It had crashed as a result of the jarring explosion. I yelled, "Get out of the house it is on fire!" I grabbed the phone as we hurried to the front door. I pulled out boots and a coat from the closet for Bob, while dialing 911.

Outside, we put the boots on and Bob said, "How can I get down the stairs?" We have six steps leading from our front door down to the sidewalk, which were very icy. I replied, "I'll get help," and ran down the snow-covered lawn to see a neighbor running towards me. As I turned around, I saw Bob at the bottom of the stairs attempting to navigate the snow. How did Bob get down those stairs? The walker was too wide for the steps. He could not sit down and scoot on his seat. Was it an angel? I tried to help him along the icy lawn.. Approximately three minutes after my exit from the car, we turned around and saw flames shooting from the roof. We were in the center of the front lawn and could hear paint cans continuing to explode. It all happened so fast. I didn't realize until that moment how close I had come to dying. The near empty tank of gas helped, but it was the hand of protection from the Lord that allowed me to flee.

We moved across the street to watch the unfolding drama. We sat on chairs on the snowy lawn with a blanket wrapped around Bob. Amazingly, the fire engines came in minutes. Not only did neighbors and people from our church arrive but the Red Cross also came with food. Somehow, Hank and Gladys Keating heard the news and came on their way home from a trip and handed us all the money they had with them. The news spread quickly and we were surrounded with well wishers. A photographer and reporter from the *Winston-Salem Journal* came to ask questions. The next day we read our story on the front page of the local section in the paper. A dramatic picture accompanied our story of a firefighter hanging out the kitchen window gasping for more air. Cell phones allowed us to alert our sons Robert and Chris at work. Our son Terry arrived as well as Jen and Annie. During this time our three grandchildren were visiting their mother and she agreed to keep them for another night. We were so grateful they had not been home taking a nap in their room right behind the garage. The stairs leading to their room were the first area the fire had traveled up to the attic. There would have been no way to reach them. The fire reached over 1600 degrees. It was so hot the vertical steel supports in the garage were bent in half. Everyone was safe and that was all that mattered.

After about three hours, the fire was under control and I was invited to go in the house with the fire chief. He tried to prepare me for what I would see. I donned a yellow hard hat and with the help of a flashlight, we surveyed the damage. As we walked through, I thought, "This isn't too bad." The living room, dining room, kitchen and guest room (Terry's) were completely devastated, but I could see many of our possessions. Later, I learned that the smoke destroys everything it touches and the cost to restore items is more than it would be to replace them. We picked up medicines, clothing, and my very smoky purse that I had tossed on the table while grabbing the phone.

We then set off for two motel rooms provided for by the Red Cross. Annie tried to clean up our blackened pill bottles before heading back to Lake Norman. Robert, Terry, Chris and Jen went to a laundramat where they did 18 loads of laundry with dismal results. Half remained spotted with black and the rest still smelled of smoke. A few items came out clean, but the rest were worthless. We slept very little that night because the strong smoke odor followed us with every item we had tried to retrieve. We awoke the next morning ready to make plans

We met with insurance agents from State Farm Insurance. They spelled out the details of the coverage. The original coverage was tied to the price we had paid for the house, not the cost of rebuilding at today's prices. Only 25% over that amount would be covered even though rebuilding would cost more. The household items coverage also had a cap. I needed to inventory the items, tell what the original cost was, and then estimate replacement cost. State Farm Insurance paid for a motel for one week so, that I could locate another place to live while the rebuilding took place. I asked about childcare for Bobby while I did all this and they agreed. The recovery process began as we moved into a suite of rooms at the Holiday Inn with a kitchenette. We were all together. The 8 of us were unharmed and ready to face the task ahead.

We had a lot of visitors at the Holiday Inn. People came with gifts for the children and food easy to serve in the motel. Someone arrived with a check for $3000. It was enough to buy a 1995 Buick LeSabre. Now we were mobile again.

I began the task of finding a home by visiting all the local apartment complexes and houses for rent. I needed space for seven or eight. I needed one large place or two close enough together and on the ground floor only, as Bob was on crutches. After three days of searching, the Lord saved the best for last. One and a half miles from our house were the Crown Park Apartments. They had two three-bedroom, 1300-square-foot apartments each on the first floor right across from each other. It even had a pool and exercise room. We were also allowed by State Farm Insurance to rent a garage to store the items we would be amassing for the new house. The apartments were unfurnished and all we had were the items Robert had moved with him from Florida. His furniture consisted of a bunk bed set and chest of drawers for the girls and a buffet. They had been in a ten-foot storage rental and these pieces were the beginning of filling the empty rooms.

Meanwhile, Julie Poplin, a local realtor whom we did not know, organized the neighbors. Julie had people call her with what they had to contribute. Ann Miller from our church volunteered to do the same thing with people from Reynolda church. Then they called to tell me what they were accruing (on paper anyway), and we said yes to everything. A young girl who knew Terry from high school decided to go house-to-house in our neighborhood and ask for money and presented us with a check for $1000. We were flabbergasted.

Friday night we opened the doors to our new apartments and the neighbors began to arrive with their donations. After they left, all eight of us plus Jen headed to Kmart as the Red Cross had given us a voucher of $100 each. It had to be spent in its entirety in one visit. I headed to the food section, and everyone else went their own way to fill their baskets. It was a huge shopping trip and a big blessing to buy food, diapers, clothing and more. We had no difficulty almost hitting our target of $800. I ran to get more diapers to utilize the entire $800 gift.

Saturday morning, one week following the fire, we arrived at our two apartments toting our few belongings and the bags from Kmart. At 8 A.M. the parade of our friends and people from Reynolda church began to arrive. It was overwhelming. Many stayed to work and distribute items to the areas they belonged in. Robert took some men to help unload his ten-foot storage area and erect the children's beds. Others filled two kitchens, six bedrooms, two living and dining rooms. At the end of a long day, the two places looked as though someone had lived there a long time. The hand of the Lord directing everyone as to what to bring was everywhere. Large items such as furniture and beds were called in to the coordinators ahead of time and planned for. Everything else was brought spontaneously. My favorite collection put together by the Lord's direction started with the arrival of a full-size headboard and frame on Friday night. On Saturday, a double mattress came followed by yellow knit sheets and pillowcases, a Laura Ashley blue and yellow comforter and shams, and a blue dust ruffle. All of these came from separate donations. Above the bed hung two pictures that blended perfectly. This was used as a guest bedroom put together by the Master Designer. Our son Terry and Jen took turns using the guest room. Both took turns coming to visit regularly during our stay at the temporary quarters.

We had four bathrooms and four sets of shower curtains including hooks. All the cupboards were filled with dishes, glasses, cooking utensils, electric appliances, and pots and pans. I am a quilter and many of my quilts were destroyed or ruined by the fire. My friend Zola Tiller came bringing a quilt she had made and quilted by hand. I do all my quilting by machine, so this was extra special to me because I knew the hours that that had been spent making it. This gift is even more special now, because Zola went home to be with Lord. Another special blessing were two coordinating sets of china, service for 14, which had belonged to a friend's mother. These sets replaced my smashed 14 place settings of Noritake china. The colors were mostly gold and I later discovered they would compliment the yellow walls in the dining room. Someone else came later with gold water goblets, which went perfectly with the china. My own grandmother's silverware had been stored in a wood chest and escaped the smoke. So when we moved back into our house, I was ready to serve dinner in beautiful style.

Peggy Tolerico, a friend from Reynolda church, spent the entire day sorting sheets, labeling the sizes, and then making each of the beds. After she left at 11 P.M., we were able to climb in our waiting bed, thank the Lord and reflect on the day. His love was so tangible as it poured out to us, under the direction of the Holy Spirit through strangers and friends. We felt loved and encouraged. Tomorrow would be soon enough to think about the difficult task of inventory.

There were many offers for continued assistance. Dinners were scheduled to arrive three times a week. Everyone seemed to bring so much food there was always enough for two days. That continued for two months. What an amazing gift to me that freed up so much time and energy, not to mention the fabulous meals that kept arriving at my door.

More volunteers came to assist with the inventory. The house was bone chilling cold and our builder brought a huge gas powered heater to help warm the space. Electric floodlights were connected to an outside temporary electric source. Most of the windows were boarded up and the basement level was totally dark. I could only be in the house for two-hour segments, as the smell would greatly irritate my membranes. Every day someone would meet me in the morning, and someone else came in the afternoon. They wrote down each item while I called them out one by one. At night I would input the information on an Excel spreadsheet. I also did research on the Internet on replacement costs, as well as what had been paid originally. It took one month and the total came to $215,000. The reason it was so high was because there were not only our things, but also Robert, Christopher and Terry's belongings. Terry had brought home from college the flannel quilt I had just completed for him. It was completely destroyed along with everything else he had lugged home for the monthlong Christmas break.

When you inventory every single CD, VCR, clothing item, things stored in the attic, toys, pantry items, toiletries, furniture, jewelry, sewing machines and accessories, it is amazing how it adds up. We would never have guessed the amount could possibly be that high. After turning in my 240-page report to State Farm Insurance, I received the good news. The loss was so much greater than the insurance coverage of $104,000 that I did not have to submit receipts and document my replacement purchases. I was so relieved! I had already divided the inventory as to what belonged to Robert, Chris and Terry. Then we prorated the amount we were given and each received their share to replace items lost. Of course our portions were not nearly enough to replace everything, but a place to begin. We encourage everyone reading this story to really assess his or her insurance coverage and consider raising the amount. We have better coverage now and it does not really cost that much more to be adequately insured. The amount of your coverage may sound adequate until you write down every item you own and add it up. Everything you own costs a lot more to replace than you can possibly imagine.

While doing the inventory, I was able to find items to save. Most precious of all were our family picture albums. They had been on a low shelf in the family room where the smoke was less dense. I bought new albums and with the help of friends, we carefully removed each picture and placed it in a new one. Even a few framed pictures were retrieved. Memories are priceless and we so enjoy looking at those "saved from the fire" pictures. They are another reminder of God's love and care for us.

My quilting friends were eager to help in some way. One afternoon, I filled large garbage bags with sacks of fabric, and quilts. They were distributed amongst the group, and washed, ironed and folded. It did not matter that the fabric had stains from the smoke that did not come out. I just have to be careful that when I cut that fabric to be used in a quilt, I need to throw away the stained parts. Some of the quilts returned were clean enough to be used, even though when I look closely I see evidence of remaining smoke.

At one time in my life I had painted with oils. The paintings that had been hanging in the house were either charred completely or covered with the black soot of ashes. I decided to take a refresher oil painting class and painted two new ones. I bought new frames and repainted the old canvases, trying to recapture what had been there. It is amazing! They do look a little different but good enough to be displayed once again on the walls.

REBUILDING ADVENTURE
(Gloria)

Finally the fun part began. I had a blank slate to plan our new house. A friend came to measure each room and the outside dimensions. Meanwhile a neighbor came over as I arrived to do the inventory. She told me a couple at her church had a fire a year ago and found a wonderful builder with the unlikely name of Gene Autry. He specialized in rebuilding houses after a fire and he had a wonderful, talented crew of workers. I called them and they invited us to see their completed house and gave me a carton of decorating and remodeling books they had used for their house. I bought a ¼ inch scale graph book and drew diagrams of each room.

The area over the garage, the living room, dining room, and kitchen were completely torn down. I asked Gene, "Could it be replaced with a vaulted ceiling in those areas?" His reply was "yes, it could be done." The original eight-foot ceilings were now raised to a center height of 14 feet. A big change was converting a bedroom to a master bath. Then the tiny bathroom area that originally served as a master bath became a closet for Bob. Bob no longer would have to travel down the hall to store his clothing. We could both fit into the bathroom at the same time and we even have two sinks! Downstairs a wall was moved out three feet, which enlarged the two bedrooms. The children's closet also grew from three feet to six feet. Three children in one room made for tight quarters and every bit of extra space was greatly appreciated.

Our friend Larry Arendas was busy building his own house at Lake Norman. However, he still made time for weekly inspection visits. He wanted to find any shoddy workmanship or materials while issues could be addressed. Larry was continually amazed at every step being completed. He never found anything he didn't approve and praise. The Lord had truly gifted us by sending someone to our door to tell us about such an experienced, fair and gifted builder. Our friend George Hoyt decided to film the process, and began filming the devastation while the house was still full of our burnt possessions. Then George came by periodically during the rebuild with his video camera. Some insurance companies suggest that you should document your belongings to have a record, should they be destroyed. I had no trouble doing most of the inventory because I could see most of our things. In the garage, where everything was reduced to ashes, it was a challenge to remember what had been there. If you do record your belongings by film or writing them down, give them to someone else for safekeeping.

Our days were filled with shopping and searching for good buys at Lowe's, Home Depot and many other building supply stores. A thick report from the insurance company documented item by item what was to be to be replaced as well as estimated replacement costs. Every item we could buy cheaper than the estimate would save money on the bottom line. If Gene went shopping, he would have just ordered or picked out the necessary item. If we took the time to comparison shop and search for the best prices, we could make a big difference. With the help of the Lord, we did just that. Every day we would pray as we left our apartment; we asked God to help us and direct our path. Some of His answers were so obviously His doing and so much fun!

Every time I went to Lowe's home improvement store, I would walk up and down the aisles looking for reduced yellow sale signs. Bob would be cruising the aisle in the motorized scooters supplied by Lowe's. One day while shopping, I could hardly believe my eyes and I hurried to find him. Every type of light fixture we needed was greatly on sale. A beautiful dining room chandelier was $28.00 marked down from $185.00. I filled a large flat bed-shopping cart with box after box of just what we needed at a fraction of the price

Gene would have paid. After five months of careful shopping, we spent $28,000.00. That amount was $20,000.00 less than the estimated amount State Farm Insurance suggested. Their estimates were usually on the bottom range of what you could spend on an item. It was no small achievement that we had saved that much. If we had let the builder just go buy what was needed, those items would have been at least $48,000.00. We thanked the Lord every day as our goal was achieved item-by-item through prayer, patience and a lot of shopping.

Another way we saved money was by doing the wallpaper and tile work. I talked Terry into working with me even though he had never done either. I had only tiled once before. We worked alongside each other through very hot, long days. We did not have a wet saw but Lowe's cut the tile for us. The foyer was easy because we only needed 10 tiles to be cut. We marked correctly and it all fit. The kitchen backsplash had four-inch tiles set on a diagonal with many obstacles to cut around. We marked and had Lowe's cut countless numbers of tiles. On the day we planned to start the kitchen, we arrived to find the plumber at the sink. We were so annoyed. Of all days he had chosen to be there in our way. As we began arranging the tiles we discovered every one needed to be cut again. A ¼ inch more needed to be cut off each tile that had already been cut. The plumber heard us of course and he said, "I have a diamond saw that you can use." He showed Terry how to use it. At the end of the day, he left the saw for us to use over the weekend so we could finish the project. We knew the Lord had sent the plumber at exactly the right time. Terry excelled in applying tiles. He wouldn't let me do the setting. He clearly did a better job and the finished project is beautiful.

Shopping for the furnishings of the house was an adventure with the Lord as well. One day I was planning the kitchen dimensions and realized I had to know the size of the refrigerator and where it would be placed. I didn't need to buy it but I needed to make a decision on size. Bob asked, "What do you want?" I replied, "I don't know, but I want the largest one I can find." After looking at every refrigerator in a large appliance store and not finding what I had hoped to find, the salesman said, "Oh, we do have one slightly dented in our back room. It is a 28-cubic-foot GE with top of the line features. The price was $2,200.00 but now it is reduced to $1,100.00." It was perfect! The spot he mentioned would be hidden so no one would ever see it. He agreed to store it until the completion of the house and deliver it for free. Everyone who sees our refrigerator comments on the little door on the front from which you can get to the milk without opening the whole door. It was a great bonus with three children. We certainly didn't need it and I did not ask for it, but the Lord was always surprising me with little touches. When we open our eyes to see God's involvement in our lives and acknowledge Him, it seems He goes out of His way to show wonderful gifts of His love. Does He need our praise and thanks? No, but I know He loves it! When we give a gift to someone it isn't done so they will thank us, but it pleases us when someone acknowledges and appreciates our gifts. The Lord does so many things in our lives that go unnoticed and unappreciated. Ask Him to open your eyes to see His loving hand.

Many of the items we had been given for the apartment went with us to the new house. Some we didn't keep and those were given to the Salvation Army. One third of our furnishings were new, one-third from the donations and one third from yard sales. What fun I had. I love the fun of the hunt for the right item at a great price. I was on my own as Bob was not able to get in and out of the car over and over without pain. Of course, I wasn't really alone. I would head out on Saturday mornings to yard sales praying and asking for God's help. Some might say, "Why would God go to a yard sale or care?" I just know He does care and did come. I usually plotted a course the night before from the newspaper ads. I was always open to deviating and relied on the Lord to direct my path.

One morning at 7 A.M., I came upon a sale that was not on my list. In their garage were many items mostly blue and yellow. Those were my color choices in many of the rooms. I made trip after trip to the car and soon I was done for the day. Bob would help me unload after these trips and wrap things up and store them in our garage. After we moved everything to our finished house, it seemed like Christmas opening all those boxes and finding just how well they all fit in. Years later, I still love to attend yard sales. Never since those days of need have I found such amazing perfect items. When the Lord is supplying your needs, He can put you at the right place at the right time. He loves to show evidence of His love and care. The God of the Universe went shopping with me and I can see evidence of His love in every corner of my home. He was able to take the resources we were given and stretch them to supply above our needs just as He said he would in the book of Philippians "My God shall supply all your needs according to His riches in glory in Christ Jesus."[1]

Many people ask me, "How did you deal with the loss?" The truth is that I focused on what I had and not what I lost. We had life, family, friends and caring evidence of a loving God. I gained a chance to rebuild an improved structure in every way. A brand new house! I was able to decorate and color with the help of the Holy Spirit. Our builder did his best to talk me into all white rooms, as it was so much easier to paint that way. I surely was not going to give up this chance to choose color. At one point in my life, I had been a personal color consultant, advising people on the best colors to wear for their particular coloring. One piece of framed art had survived because I had never removed the plastic film covering. It says, "JESUS PUTS THE COLOR IN MY LIFE," and it hangs in a new frame in our family room. I prayed, "Please help me decorate, Lord." I am so very pleased with the results of my choices.

How did He do that exactly? Many different ways, but one example is as follows: a friend asked, "What color is your family room going to be?" I answered, "I think I would like to do an Americana room, in reds, blues and creams." The next morning at a yard sale I spotted a large roll of paisley print decorator fabric in those colors. There were 20 yards for $20.00, more than enough for valances for the eight large windows in the family room. I then used all those same colors in selecting paint, wallpaper, and chairs and accessories. Ann Miller who had been the coordinator for donations from our church called one day and said, "I have a neighbor who is moving to Florida who has a couch, love seat and a coffee table. I told them about you and if you like the furniture, they will give it to you." We went and discovered the color was a perfect match for the drapes and of course we said, "YES."

Before the fire, I've never had a chance to decorate and furnish a whole house. The Lord turned that destruction of the fire and the loss of our former things into an adventure for me with Him. In Proverbs it says, "For as he thinks within himself so he is."[2] We can choose to be joyful or sorrowful. "A cheerful heart has a continual feast."[3] To me it seemed as an ever changing feast each new day. It became a daily joy to see what the Lord would provide. Today, I live in the physical reminder of those experiences. I truly do not miss what I had. His plan for us is always better. One plaque we did lose said, "God always gives the very best to those who leave the choice to Him."

DISCOURAGEMENT

It is easy and natural in a long sickness or recovery to yield to discouragement. I certainly had my moments, but I was aware most of the time the source of these thoughts were from my enemy, the devil, and endeavored to fight them off.

A month after I had somewhat recovered from my fall, I was still not able to help Gloria with the inventory. I was discouraged. I went into the garage and stood in the ashes of the fire and looked up and saw blue sky through the hole in the roof. It seemed to sink-in in a very real way, the magnitude of all our stuff gone. I lost 30 years of spiritual books, my own teachings and teachings from my mentors. Gloria had 50 one of a kind quilts either damaged or completely destroyed. The only things that survived the smoke penetration were my Bible, spiritual journals, our family pictures and a few items in storage bins. The entire weight of this happening at the same time overwhelmed me. I was discouraged. Did God really care?

I was recovering from cancer and radiation treatment, unable to eat food, a broken hip in serious pain, my son and his family living with us, my granddaughter afflicted with GBS, losing our house and 95% of everything, as well as insufficient medical and homeowners' insurance. It was overwhelming. It was crushing. I felt my whole world caving in on me. I didn't know if we could possibly recover from all these mishaps. I began to search the Psalms for comfort and understanding. What I didn't realize was that God was doing great things I could not comprehend.

When I hit bottom, a spiritual principle learned years ago bubbled to the surface—that principle is PRAISE. The power of praise during difficulties makes room for the Spirit of God to produce quality of endurance. Praise enables me to take my eyes off my circumstances and myself and to focus on the Lord Himself and His goodness. The more I praised the lighter my load felt. My spirit became buoyed and gradually praise led unto joy, which became the strength I needed to carry on.

I found comfort by reading in Psalms what King David went through in his many trials and gradually applied them to my life as I began to get God's perspective. I connected more than ever with the truth in the Psalms that David wrote when he faced his difficulties. David would comfort himself in the Lord. "This is my comfort in my affliction, that your Word has revived me."[1] All I could do was what David exhorts us to do: "Call upon Me in the time of trouble; I shall rescue you, and you will honor Me."[2]

Why was God allowing this? I knew that I was a conqueror as the word proclaims. "In all these things we overwhelmingly conquer through Him who loved us,"[3] but I certainly didn't feel like it. I felt my enemy, the devil, was buffeting me on every side. Twice in a short period of time he tried to snuff out my life, with cancer and then with the fire.

I began reflecting on the fact the Father did not spare His Son's suffering then why should I be spared? I felt I had no strength and I recalled a scripture from Corinthians. "My grace is sufficient for you, for [my] power is perfected in weakness."[4] I cried unto the Lord in my time of trouble when I felt so helpless, empty, confused and realized I didn't have the resources to put my life back together again. "I would have despaired unless I had believed that I would see the goodness of the Lord."[5] "He brought me up out of a pit of destruction, out of miry clay; and He set my feet upon a rock making my footsteps firm."[6] Gradually over time, long after I left the garage, I began to get perspective and grasp what Peter was saying, "In this you greatly rejoice even though now for a little while, if necessary you have been distressed by various trials, that the proof of your faith being much more precious than gold which is perishable, even though tested by fire, maybe found to result in praise and glory and honor at the revelation of Jesus Christ,"[7] and what Paul writes in Romans, "For I consider that the sufferings of this present time are not worthy to be compared with the glory that is to be revealed to us."[8]

Over time I could rejoice that God's plan was to enrich and beautify me through these problems, to expose my weakness and hidden sins of self-centeredness, self-reliance and pride. For this I am deeply appreciative. I thank God He used these circumstances to humble me. He was working on perfecting faith in me, which produces the quality of endurance. It has prepared the soil of my heart for fresh growth in goodness that both God and I want.

Yes, all our stuff was gone, but it was only stuff. It could be replaced. The important things were not touched. We were all living. I could be visiting Gloria in the burn unit of the hospital or the cemetery. God was so good to spare our lives.

The car that exploded was a Chrysler product. The leaking valve had already been replaced because of a recall. Obviously the replaced valve was not any better than the one they had recalled. I began the process of filing a claim against Chrysler. After writing letters and getting legal council, I was told I could never win a lawsuit because there was no loss of life and Chrysler would bury me in legal costs. The lawsuit couldn't be just damages to the car and destruction of our house. It would have to be for millions of dollars before a team of lawyers would represent me. Before giving up the idea, I tried one last approach. I wrote a soft, gentle letter to the chairman of Chrysler with a short description of the incident, appealing for Chrysler to do the right thing and give me a new car. I never heard from them. Needless to say, I will never buy another Chrysler again.

As I have given my testimony, people say that it sounds like a story from the book of Job. Well, there are similarities.[9]

- Job lost his livestock, which was his way of making a living.
  I lost my job, which was my way of making a living.
- Job lost his health
  I lost my health
- Job had a big wind come and destroy his house

We had a fire destroy our house
- Job had boils
  I had 21 sores in my mouth.
- Job had three friends who hounded him about how there must be sin in his life.
  I had three friends who accused me of lack of faith or sin in my life.
- Job knew the sweetness of the Presence of God and also perceived absences of God for a season during his suffering.
  Likewise, I had the same experiences.
- Job was urged to curse God, but never did.
  I wasn't tempted that way, but I kept asking in prayer. God helped me make the right responses to these circumstances.
- Job had his fortunes restored double fold.
Likewise, we had our fortunes restored double fold.

Two differences between Job and me were, that I didn't lose my children and I am not going to live to be 140 years old!

The "Why" Question

In the back of my mind, and I suspect many others,' when deep troubles come knocking on our door it is easy to ask the "Why?" question. "Why me, O God? Don't you love me anymore? There must be sin in my life. Is this God's punishment for my sinful past? Why now?" Maybe that is the wrong question. Maybe the question should be "Why not me?" Does it really matter that my circumstances are difficult? My question comes from a different perspective. I believe the "Why?" question is offensive to God because it challenges God with what is behind the question. God, if you really knew what You were doing, You would not do this to your children. Why would you take a small child in a horrible death before they had a chance to live life? Or, why would you allow this child to have a long horrible disease? I fully realize these types of questions are much deeper than my "Why?" question.

I wouldn't presume to have answers, but I do know some problems are too big for me to carry. What has been helpful to me in handling the "Why?" question is an excerpt from Corrie Ten Boon's book, *The Hiding Place*.[A1] The scene is when Corrie and her father are on the train headed to the big city to buy clock parts. Corrie is about eight years old when she asks her father about sex. About that time they reach their destination. Her father wisely asks Corrie to carry his suitcase. She tries, but can't because it is too heavy. Her father says, "Corrie let me carry it for now. When you are older and stronger then you can." He says, "It is the same thing about your sex question. You are not old enough or strong enough to carry that question now. Let your father handle it until you are ready." Many times I have had to tell my heavenly Father that that there are things I cannot carry. Such as deaths I don't understand, or an unfair judgment that is too heavy for me to carry. You carry it until I am older and stronger and wiser. Sometimes heavy problems must be left in the mighty hands of our heavenly Father. I am convinced that one-day when I get to heaven those difficult questions will be answered. Maybe some of them will be answered before I get to heaven. Until then, when there are no clear answers, I just let God be God and trust Him that this tragedy fits into a bigger picture. It fits His purposes and plan. One day, we all will have the answers to the difficult questions.

WILDERNESS EXPERIENCE

The Lord opened my eyes to see a valuable lesson on balance. About a year after my melt down in the garage, I had a spiritual high mountain top experience with the Lord. My hip pain had subsided, my teaching on the tabernacle in Sunday school class was going well and I felt satisfaction in being able to contribute again. My quiet prayer times in the morning were rich with the Lord. Spiritual life can be represented as a +1 in the following way:

Mountaintop: +1 Balance: 0 Spiritual funk: — 1

Within two weeks, I developed a terrible spiritual funk. A real frustration in my spirit and body developed. Everything going great was not going great any more. I couldn't drink anything by mouth, so I was back on the tube 100%. The teaching tapes weren't coming out, and I believed God was calling us and many other churches to repent and spend time in corporate prayer for the sins of the country, but we weren't responding. My spirit was in intercession for the country as everyone else wanted to talk about how good God is.

What I learned from this quick drop going from +1 to a –1 is a lesson on mountaintop experiences and crushed grapes and how God uses both to grow us in intimacy. I don't live on the mountaintop; I go there. It might be a retreat center, a getaway spiritual oasis, or just a period of well-being sensing God's involvement in my Life. I don't experience permanent residence in the Holy Place in the tabernacle; I go there for spiritual refreshment, worship, spiritual guidance, and adoration. I leave there to live outside the tabernacle in the camp. It is in the camp where I apply what I have learned in the Holy Place. It is out there, down in the valley, that I apply what I learned in the Presence of the Lord in the Holy of Holies. It is out there; God has me between His index finger and thumb and crushes the grape to bring forth a sweet wine. It is out there, He teaches me how to be broken bread and poured-out wine with which to feed and nourish others. It is where the balance between +1, 0, –1 stays in focus. God doesn't want me to camp on either the mountaintop or wallow in a spiritual funk. Maturity will be achieved if I can balance at ground zero.

I have been blessed to tell of my cancer experience in a number of churches in this country and others. When I give my testimony, the question is usually asked, "What was the most difficult part of the ordeal?" My immediate answer is the "Wilderness Experience."

Going through these events, I experienced the full range of emotions not only physically but also spiritually and emotionally. I had battles with discouragement, disappointment, and impatience regarding the time it took to recover. How long was this going to take? I cried out to the Lord for His grace to get me through just one more day.

In the beginning, I experienced His Presence in a very real way. The time surrounding the major operation was a unique spiritual blessing. I can't find words to express it. He came along side of me by the power of His Holy Spirit as I was going through the operations. I was flooded with peace and had absolutely no doubt the outcome. It was marvelous. For many years, I have known the presence of the Lord and the sweetness of experiencing Him and His manifest presence.

However, about the time of the radiation and on through the hip ordeal the Lord's Presence withdrew. It is described in the Song of Solomon. "I sought Him but did not find Him."[1] He was there all the time behind the latticework, silent. My prayers seemed to bounce off the ceiling. I was spiritually cold. I could not pray, read my Bible, or focus on the Lord. I had not backslid. I knew God loved me and saw me through the operations and was blessing us in wonderful ways. He was hidden behind the latticework. I could not reach Him. I felt naked and alone.

Heavy medication and pain prevented me from focusing or concentrating. The pain was all-absorbing. I would be groggy and dopey. It went on for a long time; it was terrible. Looking back, it was probably the worst part of the trial. It made me realize what a tremendous gift His presence is in my life and how much I depend upon it daily. I feel empty, alone, and dirty without Him.

I continued to cry out to Him that I knew the scripture, which says, "He will never leave me, nor forsake you,"[2] but why didn't He answer me sooner with His divine presence and warmth? The only conclusion I could come up with was that He was testing me to see if I would continue to seek His face or was I only interested in receiving from His hand that which comes in the form of blessings?

After a long dry spiritual season things changed and like King Solomon wrote, "He has made everything beautiful in its time."[3]

When His presence returned I enjoyed His sweet fellowship again. It was like a fresh shower after a long, hot, sweaty day in the field.

His absence helped me realize how much I missed Him when He was gone, and how I can take Him for granted and can be careless with this gift. His presence is like honey in the rock, the sweetness of the Rose of Sharon and is worth more than gold or silver. His silence was a sign that He was bringing me into an even more wonderful understanding of Himself.

Added to the Lord's absences during this time, members of the church withdrew. It can happen when compassionate people really have empathy for the situation yet don't know what to say after awhile. After they asked me, "How are you doing?" 50 times and there was no improvement, they felt awkward and stopped asking. So they stopped coming around to visit and ducked to avoid me at church. It was like all of a sudden I had leprosy. What it did in one sense was create a feeling of loneliness. In another sense, when I was really sick it took too much energy to give them an accurate answer. Also, I would get tired of repeating myself. That is why the Internet is so great. I could say it once then circulate it to people asking. I know of other cancer patients using this tool of communication more often and more effectively than I did.

Nonetheless, the days would crawl by with no conversation outside of family. I am sure my Father, as a part of the "Wilderness experience," engineered it. As I have ministered to other cancer patients, some have mentioned the same thing. If you are ministering to a very sick person, don't abandon them. Come along side often and sit awhile even if only a few words are expressed. Just being there is a big boost.

FAVOR OF THE LORD

Those were the circumstances surrounding our trials. Now let me share what God did with those circumstances. I prayed to the Lord to heal me miraculously, to deliver me from the cancer and surgery, and the sciatic pain. That was not His immediate plan. Why? It was not God's purpose. He had things to show me; sin to rout out of my life. He had a much bigger agenda than just healing. He wanted to change my direction, my life, my priorities, and my focus. So He did it in such a way to get my attention as well as achieve His purposes. "For my thoughts are not your thoughts. Neither are your ways My ways declares the Lord. For as the heavens are higher than the earth, so are My ways higher than your ways, and My thoughts higher than your thoughts."[1] His ways are absolutely amazing!

After surgery, pain, and suffering trials and tribulation for two and half years, one day the God of the universe swept down into my broken life with His miraculous power and touched me. Instantly healing came into my body. O' the wondrous power of the blood of Jesus to heal our broken bodies. At a Sunday service God chose to move mightily. Sunday September 1, 2002 HE HEALED ME AND MIRACULOSLY TOUCHED ME! Why that day, when many times before people had laid hands on me and gathered around and prayed? I don't know! He chose September 1 to touch me. Pastor Alan Wright wasn't teaching about healing and no one was praying for me. As we were in the midst of worship, He touched me! It was the "fullness of time" To God Be The Glory! I was touched by the Spirit of God and knew it immediately. I experienced a warm glow from God's manifested presence. After the service, people came up to me and asked what was happening to me. They could see God was at work all over me. I didn't want to leave the pew but I knew God touched me and I couldn't keep it to myself. I began going around telling people I was healed. The first thing I noticed was that I HAD SALIVA FLOWING IN MY MOUTH AGAIN FROM SALIVA GLANDS THAT WERE REMOVED. After two and half years with no saliva and it just started to flow. It was a creative miracle. One moment there was no saliva, the next moment it was flowing. Soon, I no longer had to carry my water bottle with me sipping every two or three minutes. Oh how wonderful it is to moisten your lips with your tongue. Since then, the flow has been restored 100%. Today I carry a water bottle not out of need but because I learned to enjoy water so much. I always like to have some available. In fact, the only thing I drink today is water or coffee. It is so good being able to spit again! My teeth were miraculously preserved. I didn't lose one tooth, which is extraordinary according to my dentist. That much radiation shot at the jaw and throat area always puts the teeth in jeopardy.

I went to have an endoscopy and the doctor stretched my esophagus to a normal size. The ulcer on my esophagus disappeared. Although I had already begun eating many things after September 1 because the saliva had returned, I now was able to eat everything placed in front of me. My appetite was restored and my taste buds returned. I was like a kid in the candy store. I would see a Krispy Kreme donut or a Snickers bar and remember how good it was and savor the taste. It was even better than I remembered. I thoroughly enjoyed eating. I couldn't get enough garlic bread. It was amazing how much more I enjoyed eating than ever before. I had ice cream every day. I had steak and hot dishes and, nothing was a problem. I could eat everything and didn't put on weight. It was marvelous.

An incredible miracle took place in my prayer room directly above where the fire was the hottest. Everything in that area was totally lost except my spiritual journal and Bible. Both the Bible and the journal survived the flames, smoke and the water. The Bible came through without a mark on it. The journal was marred and sooty on the outside, but not one word was lost. Like in the book

of Daniel "The fire had no effect on the bodies of these men, ...
nor had the smell of fire even come upon them."[2] So it was with my
Bible today. Ann Miller took my Bible and aired it out page-by-page
and allowed the sun to shine upon it. Today there is absolutely no
evidence the Bible went through a fire and has absolutely no smell
of smoke. I still use that same Bible every day. It was a miracle!

IT IS GREAT TO BE ALIVE.
IT IS GREAT TO BE ABLE TO EAT.
IT IS GREAT NOT TO BE IN PAIN.
IT IS GREAT TO GET UP EVERY MORNING AND
CELBRATE ANOTHER DAY ON PLANET EARTH.

Doris Russell arrived at the apartment bearing many gifts. One
was a brand new TV with a built in VCR so the children could watch
videos. She asked me, "What size are you, Bob?" Her son-in-law
was a public speaker and owned a large wardrobe because of his job.
Doris returned several days later with armloads of clothes. All of my
clothes with the exception of a few items stored in an enclosed barrel
had been destroyed. I was gifted with suits, sport coats, sweaters,
jackets, shirts and pants. All fit perfectly. That is not easy as I am 43
long, which is not a common size. There were so many clothes that
Robert and Chris were also able to choose some things as well.

One of the simple pleasures of life so important to our welfare is
a good night's sleep. Much is written about the benefits a good eight
hours of sleep has on many aspects of living. Conversely, there are
detrimental effects of insufficient sleep. I learned how true that was
and to this day my sleeping is unusual.

As I mentioned before, I could not lie down to sleep for two and
half years due to a dry mouth caused by no saliva. Whenever I lay
down, my nose would clog up and I would have to sleep with my
mouth open. That made my dry mouth worse. What a relief when
the Lord suddenly restored my saliva by miraculously creating new
saliva glands. However, that is not the end of my sleeping story.
Now with an eight-inch plate in my right hip I could not sleep on my
right side during the night due to discomfort or pain. I had to sleep
with a pillow between my legs every night. I could not sleep flat on

my back or stomach because of the scar tissue in my throat and jaw. I had only my left side to sleep on all night in the same position. That was not good.

Since we needed new beds after the fire, this was the perfect time to purchase beds that could electronically be raised or lowered. We bought beds with Tempur-Pedic mattresses made with memory foam. The only way I can sleep today is slightly elevated on my back or on my left side. When we travel, I prop two or three pillows on the headboard behind my head so I can sleep with my head elevated. One of the great blessings that occurred because of the fire came a solution to finally sleeping well. God has gifted me, in spite of these inconveniences, with the pleasure of a deep, full eight hours of sleep nightly. It is just another way God cares for me. It emphasizes the scripture in Proverbs which says, "When you lie down, you will not be afraid: When you lie down your sleep will be sweet"[3]

My sciatic nerve problem that occurred after the broken hip ceased to be a focal point and the pain has been reduced to the point of no longer being a preoccupation. I have a repaired hip and I can function again. I am trusting God for the total recovery. I am not completely healed today, but I am one day closer.

My incurable skin disease Rosacea was healed completely. The doctors said there was no cure for it but it could be treated for the rest of my life with prescriptions. Little did they know the power of my healing Jesus? I no longer needed expensive prescriptions or creams on my face. It is all gone. It is the grace of God.

Not being able to eat solid food for two and half years meant I could not participate in a communion service. I am one of the people who pass out communion to the congregation. It was extremely difficult serving other people communion but having to pass on it myself. I was concerned the first time I took communion after being able to swallow water. I was fearful I would not be able to get down the bread of communion. Although it felt like a knife as it passed down my throat, I did not choke. A few minutes later when the juice was passed it did help wash down the bread. What a marvelous blessing, to once again participate with the Body of Christ, as it is such a significant part of my life. Never again will I take communion casually.

The miracles were not because of anything I can take credit for, nor any minister or single prayer warrior laying hands on me at the time of the miracle. I believe God heard all the many prayers of the saints and sent the healing. The doctors couldn't take credit for the miracles either. They were mystified particularly when I told them Jesus healed me. I had excellent medical care. All of the medical staff was wonderful. I appreciated everyone. They all did what they were trained to do. But they were only instruments of God. None of them could produce saliva, heal the skin disease, or enable the esophagus to be stretched again to normal size. IT WAS MY JESUS. My healing was not based upon my agony, but the agony of Jesus on the cross and His redemptive grace. He is the Great Physician, the maker of our bodies and the healer when they break down. Praise His Mighty Name. It was His grace in the fullness of time.

"But thou, O Lord, are merciful and gracious, God, slow to anger and abundant in loving kindness and truth."[4]

The outpouring of love expressed by family and friends touched me deeply. Our good friends Larry and Carole Arendas changed their plans and drove up from Charlotte to be with me during the operation, along with pastor Alan Wright. My brother Terry, my sister Jeannine, and her husband Alan, drove from Kansas City to be with me while recovering from the radiation. My six children were a deep source of ministry to both of us.

My youngest son, Terry, changed his summer plans to come along side and take care of me and help with the chores. My oldest son, Robert, lived with us and has always been at my side and has been a faithful servant fixing everything that needed to be fixed. He has now moved out of our house after living with us for six years. He married Christina who has an eight-year-old daughter named Kenzie. We have been blessed with another grandchild. They are only a block away and Robert is still at my right hand, serving when needed. My other children and spouses, Sherri, Scott and Amanda, David and Natalie were out of the area but were very loving, caring and concerned. Their circumstance prevented them from being physically here but their love and concerns were a great comfort.

It is not until you are on the receiving end of prayers that you experience the full expression from love of the Body of Christ.

Prayers, cards, and food were supplied for weeks and weeks. Words of comfort, scriptures and encouragement overwhelmed us. Members of Reynolda church and other saints met our every need, demonstrating as scripture promises "And my God shall supply all your needs according to His riches in glory in Christ Jesus."[5]

Carole and Larry Arendas's grandchildren Kathryn and Christopher were only three and five years old when they started to pray for me that I would be able to eat spaghetti again. They continued every night and prayed for two and a third years. They stopped only after they heard the good news that I could once again eat spaghetti. Many people we didn't know or had never met before prayed for us. I think I hold the record for being on the "prayer needs list" the longest at church. For three years the saints faithfully prayed for me. When I did start eating again, I could watch out of the corner of my eye people watching me eat. A number of them told me it gave them great pleasure to watch me eat again after watching me pour the vanilla junk into my tube for over two years.

Previously, I had published a book called *Executive Job Search Strategies* [B-1] that was distributed throughout the United States and other countries on how to get a job. I had written a second book that was ready to be sent to prospective publishers. Then the fire struck. It not only completely destroyed all of the copies of my first book in the house, but also the second book. Everything on the computer hard drive was completely destroyed, all back-up copies and all written drafts. All of the research and over a year of writing were gone! I said, "Lord I guess you don't want that book to go forth. When You send a message you send a strong one!" I didn't know what He had in mind was for Gloria and me to write this book five years later. Once again it was in the fullness of time.

My cancer bills amounted to approximately $200,000 which was 100% covered by COBRA insurance from my previous employer Wachovia. There is a requirement for employers to carry severance employees on their insurance program for 18 months after being laid off. You have to pay the premium but it is usually much less then getting insurance on your own. My last medical follow-up appointment for cancer was in the last month I was eligible for COBRA. The entire bill was covered. The only portion I paid was a few $15 co-pays and my monthly premium.

God surely provided the money for my cancer through COBRA. In addition, He faithfully provided for the medical bills concerning my hip through the people at Reynolda church. I did not have to pay anything out of pocket; the church covered all the expenses what insurance didn't cover. I was still faced with paying the builder from my homeowners insurance. My homeowners insurance was insufficient to cover rebuilding expenses. The builder tried his best to rebuild the house with our insurance coverage, but due to the increased cost of materials he couldn't do it.

My brother Terry was the priest for two small middle class churches in Missouri. He told them about our trials one Sunday at Mass and asked them to pray for us. He intentionally made no mention of the money situation. The next week they took a collection for us, then a second, and then a third. One of their collections for me was greater than the money they needed to operate the church that week. The gift from my brother's church, added to the reimbursement from the insurance company, totaled enough to pay Gene Autry in full. The amount they sent was exactly what was needed to cover the extra rebuilding cost. These people didn't know me, knew nothing about me except to hear about our circumstances, but generously poured out their love, cards and money. They sent $15,881.00, exactly what we needed to finish the job. I didn't have a mortgage before the fire and I did not need one after the restoration. To God be the glory!

As the psalmist says, "Unless the Lord builds the house, they labor in vain who build it."[6] But when the Lord builds the house, it is awesome. After you live in a house for a while you realize its deficiencies. Well, we had the opportunity to change it any way we wanted to as long as we stayed within the footprint of the original foundation. We moved walls, increased room sizes, added new storage space and many other improvements. The house today has seven major improvements. Five years later, there is not one thing we would change about the house. All our needed improvements were accomplished.

Family, friends, and my relatives the Carneys from Wichita, Kansas contributed $4500. All together $39,026 came in through the generosity of family, church friends, neighbors, and relatives, and people in Missouri. It was all directed by the love of the Holy Spirit. Praise God, He is outrageous in His blessings!

Earlier in the book I wrote about the "why?" question. Now I want to revisit the "why?" question from a different perspective. Why us? Why would we be chosen to experience the favor of the Lord in so many profound experiences? The miracles God worked in our lives overwhelm us. We are in awe that God would visit us with such a privilege. What words of thanks can we possibly return to Him for these trials and the blessings that followed? Yes, there was a price to pay, but the blessings far exceed the trials. Those trials have changed our lives forever. They were the gateway for the double fold blessings that followed, which are awesome. But even greater is the realization the God of the universe would care. He who created the billion of stars and multitudes of galaxies would care enough for us in such a minuscule detail as to give us coordinating curtain rods and all the other multitude blessings that are so insignificant in the big picture. He has showered blessings upon us. Why us O God? It is truly humbling.

The improvements were not only in the house but also more importantly in us. There were so many lessons and wisdom gained through these years as you will see in the next chapter.

WISDOM GAINED

Now that time has passed, I see more clearly some of what the God was trying to accomplish in me and through me. With more understanding, I appreciate the scripture which says "All things work together for those that love God, to those who are called according to His purpose."[1]

I don't know anybody who has a near death experience that comes out of it the same person. It changed my perspective on just about everything. The first thing I try to do when I get up in the morning is CELEBRATE another day and try to live life with gusto, savoring how precious my "NOT YET" time is on earth. I appreciate all of creation far more than previously. It is good to be alive. It changed my values as to what is important: 1) God, 2) family, 3) health, and 4) ministry. Previously, I was caught up in many things including political issues, financial deals and investment matters. At one point, I was the State of Massachusetts representative for the Freedom Council of Christian Broadcasting Network. Although they are all good pursuits, I now find them to be a distraction from the four main focuses of life.

> "I AM RESOLVED NO LONGER TO LINGER,
> CHARMED BY THE WORLD'S DELIGHT;
> THINGS THAT ARE HIGHER,
> THINGS THAT ARE NOBLER,
> THESE HAVE ALLURED MY SIGHT."[C-1]

What a great adventure life is. I have learned God is much bigger than I ever realized. I can't put Him in a box or reduce Him to fit in my little box of understanding.

God doesn't call bad what we call bad or evil. God calls gossip, murmuring, worry, and doubt bad. We call what happened to me bad. It is not bad at all! It was the tool the potter used to shape me the way He wanted me, not the way I thought He should shape me. I am being shaped according to His vision and plan not mine. Much has happened to me over the past eight years, none of which is bad. Whatever happens to me, God can take my situation and weave His redemptive work to accomplish His purpose in His time.

More than one person has asked:

> Did God give you cancer?
> Did God burn down your house?
> Did God cause you to fall?

To get the answer to those questions we need to look at the scriptures in the book of Job. In chapter one, Satan is allowed to test Job. God gives Satan permission for all those tribulations to occur, but not to take Job's life. God knows Job's heart and knows the outcome of the encounter before it begins. God knew the outcome; Satan did not! "Behold, how happy is the man whom God reproves, so do not despise the discipline of the Almighty."[2] Job went through much pain, anguish and sorrow, but the end of the story is what movies are made of. He lived happily ever after. He was far better off than before the ordeal. That in a nutshell is our testimony.

God allowed these things to happen, just like He allowed Satan to test Job. Bob, "are you saying God who is totally loving allows hurtful things to happen to His children?" In the words of his book, *Prepare to Meet Your God* [D-1] my friend, pastor Glenn Pearson writes, "Strange as it may seem to our way of thinking God actually does use hardship, afflictions, and suffering to forge and impact character transformation into believers who trust Him." Scripture speaks for itself on this point. God is speaking very clearly in the book of Peter when He states, "Beloved do not think it strange concerning the fiery ordeal among you, which comes upon you for your testing as though some strange thing were happening to you."[3] God is the Master Designer and He allows adversities into your and my life to see if we can jump over them properly. As the psalmist says, "By my God I can leap over a wall."[4] He was with us in the midst of our circumstances. He planned how He would get the glory through our circumstances There is no way I or any other person could take credit for any of it. Neither the doctor nor prayer warriors can take the credit. He did not want man to get the glory lest they boast. The dealings or blessings that followed, to God alone be the glory. He knew what He would accomplish through these trials and how He could use it. God didn't change my circumstances. He wanted to achieve His purposes as He changed me in the midst of my circumstances. And that He did!

We live in a fallen world. In the book of John, Jesus says "the thief (the devil) comes to steal, and kill, and destroy: I came that they might have life, and might have it abundantly."[5]

God did not burn down my house; a faulty engine part caused the fire. God did not push me over so I would fall down and fracture my hip. I broke my hip because I was clumsy and lost my balance and fell to the concrete. What God did was redeem these problems so blessings would come out of them. Sometimes He prevents things from happening. We have many stories we could share not related to these trials. Sometimes he allows it, and other times He cleans up the messes we get ourselves in because of our sin, weakness, and yielding to the devil's temptations. In each trial His love and compassion were at work if I could only see it.

What Jesus Did for Me:

JESUS delivered Gloria from a fiery situation or death.
JESUS kept the grandchildren away from the fire.
JESUS supplied two perfect apartments for eight months.
JESUS provided an excellent builder who exceeded our expectations
JESUS built us a new house and furnished it.
JESUS delivered me from death <u>twice.</u>
JESUS restored my saliva glands, taste buds and appetite.
JESUS healed me so I could eat again.

JESUS healed my Rosacea an incurable skin disease.

JESUS restored my sleep, enabling me to lie down on my left side.

JESUS supplied our financial needs from local people as well as from others 1,500 miles away.

JESUS gave us a double portion of financial blessings.

JESUS paid my medical bills when I had inadequate insurance.

JESUS paid my building costs when I had inadequate insurance.

JESUS supplied encouragement through prayers, cards and care.

JESUS gave Gloria great grace, strength, and courage.

JESUS took away our fear and anxiety.

JESUS provided excellent medical professionals.

JESUS supplied finances for the past eight years equal to my last Salary at the bank

This list is not complete but it sure brings to light the scripture, which says "Now to Him who is able to do exceeding abundantly beyond all we ask or think, according to the Power that works within us to Him be the glory."[6]

My experiences have scared some people. More than one person has expressed such thoughts. One friend said, "Bob, if I had to go through what you went through, I am not sure I would remain a Christian." I couldn't find the proper words to share with them. It is not poor ole' Bob. I look back on our trials as one of the greatest blessings I have experienced in my life. Don't get the wrong idea. I never want to repeat even one aspect of the dealing—ever. But, the blessings that have flowed since then have been marked all over with the favor of the Lord. Even today, the favor is so present and real, not only in my life and Gloria's but also in each of the 27 family members in my Bruce clan. Like Job, we have truly received a double portion of God's blessings.

God gave me the scripture in Luke which says, "Simon, Simon, behold Satan has demanded permission to sift you like wheat; but I have prayed for you, that your faith would not fail; and you, when once you have been restored again strengthen your brothers."[7] Since my recovery, I have had the opportunity to pray and encourage many other cancer patients. Many have listened to the tape of the testimony. The miracles God did for me are an encouragement to others. I have been blessed to share my testimony many times here in this country. In 2002, Hank, Mickey and I were ministering in South Africa and I was giving my testimony while still on the feeding tube. They had never seen or heard of such a thing. It had an amazing impact on them. It was on that trip that my eight-ounce cans of nourishment were lost in transit. We landed and all the baggage was there except my suitcase filled with cans. They were so concerned and dismayed when they found out I couldn't eat any of their food. I couldn't buy my cans there, as it was a prescription formula that they did not have. I had an emergency stock in my flight bag along with extra cans in Mickey and Hank's suitcases. Two days later, my luggage caught up and I had plenty of cans. Gloria and I joined Hank in Bulgaria in 2004 and again in South Africa in 2005. They, too, greatly rejoiced to see me eat without my feeding tube.

You may recall one of my first prayers was for God to increase the size of my mustard seed. He did it! One of God's purposes was to grow my Faith. Once you believe you have heard from God to act, your actions require immediate obedience. Faith does not tolerate procrastinating, common sense reasoning, or understanding the outcome before beginning. We experienced this twice. First, in buying a six-bedroom house when we didn't need a house that large. Secondly, to stop working immediately when God said I was finished working for the secular world. This is never easy to do and provides a real down-to-earth test of living faith. In both cases we were sure we heard from God so we acted. We have learned to never doubt in darkness what we knew to be true in the light:

> ➤ "Without faith it is impossible to please Him."[8]
> ➤ I had to cling to faith during my darkest hour.
> ➤ These experiences have strengthened our faith.
> ➤ I know Him better now than before this happened.
> ➤ Faith must be tried.
> ➤ I know His love for Bob Bruce and all that has happened has been in His plan —none of this slipped by Him and the

plan He has for me is "Thoughts of peace not of evil to give {me} a future and a hope."[9]

➢ I am learning faith is built on building blocks.
➢ By faith, we glorify God.
➢ By faith, we strengthen each other.
➢ By faith, we appreciate how much we need help with our frailty.
➢ By faith, we are kept humble.
➢ By faith, we can move the mountains in our lives.

I also realized the enemy of faith is murmuring, doubt, fear, discouragement and worry. The trick is not to fall into the trap of self-pity or indulge in the luxury of misery. The sin of self-pity is ugly because it removes God from the center of life and replaces Him with self-interest. These were some of the devil's favorite arrows in his quiver to bring me down. He was quick to launch his arsenal at me with these negatives.

I have learned in the time of anxiety not to listen to the lies and snares of the evil one who whispers: "You have no faith, there is no hope for you." Jesus did not call me to have faith in my faith or faith in healing. He did say even in my weakness He would show Himself strong on my behalf. He is not looking for me to have faith in a formula, or in a promise book. I do not need to have faith in miracles. I need faith in the One who works miracles. I do not need faith in healing. I need faith in the One who heals. He is attempting to teach me to have absolute faith in Him and His goodness. As long as I have the idea that God will always bless me in answer to prayers, He will do it.

In addition to faith it is important to understand the value of supernatural hope. If you are fighting cancer or some other terminal health condition cling to hope. Hope for strength and overcoming grace and power for healing. Hope is the strongest antidote against discouraging medical reports. When you are discouraged the way the disease is progressing, or how slowly you are recovering from chemotherapy or radiation be strengthen by scriptures about healing. Look them up, memorize them, and recite them often. You will find some in chapter three of this book. There is a great power in supernatural hope. Not a human hope, but rather hope in Jesus the hope of the world. The hope found in the atonement work of Jesus on the cross; the hope in the absolute goodness of God. Cling to hope until your last breath. With hope comes a peace of mind that is not natural. It is a peace that passes understanding.

Why did God set aside a season of testing for us? So we could have a more wonderful understanding of Him. God wasn't concerned with my plans. He didn't ask me if this was a convenient time to have some difficulties. He didn't ask if I wanted to go through these trials. God allowed these difficulties to see if I would become better or bitter. If the Father did not spare His only Son from unimaginable suffering no other person has ever experienced, then why should I be excused from suffering?

Somewhere along the line, I began to realize it was all an elaborate set up. God did not cause my problems but His redemptive grace turned these events from something horrible into magnificent blessings.

God is sovereign. Everything that happens to me is either Allowed or caused by my loving Father for my good and His glory.

He allowed all the details, engineered the circumstances, the problems, and tribulations very carefully. From the foundation of time He knew what He was doing. He saw the beginning, middle and the end of the trial. He knew the responses I would make, the prayers and the suffering before it happened. He sets it up so I could grow in the image of His Son, and pressed many people into praying for my recovery. The results would be bountiful, outrageous blessings whereby He could receive the glory and we would have our socks blessed off!

Although all of these circumstances seemed to hit close together, God knew about them and worked them into His plan to draw me to Himself. What is amazing, I had exactly zero input into these difficulties. I could not have seen, anticipated, or done anything different to avoid them. I could not manipulate the circumstances. Each was done unto me and all were beyond my control.

Going through the trials, I tried to stay focused. I continually asked my Father to help me make the right response to each situation. I prayed diligently that I would not step into any of the devil's manholes, snares, or entrapments; that I would not go down the path of his lies or temptations to curse God for my trials. Admittedly, when I first received the diagnosis, I fell into some of the above traps, including the "What if" thinking. These destructive thoughts destroy faith, hope, trust, and belief that God is the healer.

As I look back on those years, a key point has emerged. What was obscured and veiled at the time has now become increasingly clear. What did God want to accomplish through all the drama? It was a set up to bring me to the end of my rope and to reach some very deep issues in my life. I am sure He tried to reach me through other means, but I missed His nudging. It was only by going through, not by taking the by-pass road around the suffering, that these truths became evident.

Earlier in this chapter I talked about being disciplined by the Lord. Being disciplined has nothing to do with any wrongdoing but wrong thinking in my life. It has to do with reduction of my independence. It reaches into the very depth of my being and crucifies my self-life the right to my own ways. It removes my propensity towards self-sufficiency. The end result of the disciplining is to make me more useful to Him in the out working of His purposes.

God was exposing major sins in my life titled self-dependence, self-reliance and pride. He showed me the nature of my sin was rooted in my claim to my right to myself, to be able run my own life. I wanted to rely upon my intelligence, training, and education to manage my life. In other words, to be the boss of my life rather than to surrender fully to Him and let Him be the boss of all aspects of my life. He wanted me to know how deeply these sins were rooted into my being and to confess and repent for them. Without the trials, this cornerstone truth would have continued to hide in obscurity. For this revelation, I will be eternally grateful.

YOUR OWN TRIALS

Have you ever noticed how troubles often seem to come in bunches? Difficult situations bunched close to each other. In our case, we had six difficult trials:

However, those were our trials. Your situation is surely different. I don't know what trials you are presently facing. I am sure they are different than ours. Regardless of what you are facing, I can promise you two things. The first is you will face trials in this life. This is not a promise from me, but from Jesus Himself. He said, "In this world you have tribulation, but take courage; I have overcome the world."[1] Trials accomplish a purpose in your life; it is to conform you to the image of Jesus. In Romans we read, "We also exult in our tribulation, knowing that tribulation brings about perseverance; and perseverance, proven character; hope; and hope does not disappoint, because the love of God poured out within our hearts through the Holy Spirit who was given to us."[2]

In the middle of that scripture, are the words, "proven character." They are easy to miss. Through trials, the Father is developing our character to be like Jesus. Trouble is a tool God uses to bring us to Himself, mature us, and grow and develop character. God allows troubles to reach us in areas we are not willing to change on our own and to break self-sufficient attitudes. "God is a refuge and a strength a very present help in trouble."[3]

So, maybe you are in a season where life is fine. The sun is shining brightly and everything is going along great as the bumper sticker says: "Life is Good." Don't get to comfortable. Things at some point will change so you can be blessed with trials.

The second is a promise that Jesus will see you through your trials. "God is faithful, who will not allow you to be tempted beyond what you are able."[4] You may just think you do not have the strength to get through this trial. His promise is that "The righteous cry out and the Lord hears, and delivers them out of all their troubles."[5] But you say Bob; you don't know what I am going through. My troubles are worse than yours. My answer to you is the same. Jesus will see you through and in the fullness of time you will come out the other end of the trial. Your trial may be health, stage four cancer, children on drugs, abuse, pain, disappointment, death of a loved one, or maybe one of 100 different things. The answer is always Jesus. Trust, believe and have faith in Jesus, His redemptive grace, His Word, and you will come out of your situation stronger than when you went in. Suffering is for a season.

God is good all the time. Even in the darkest hour, His light will shine. His Word is true. He is faithful to His Word.

Our hope in writing this book is to offer you hope in your situation. To help you realize God cares about you and what you are going through. He will give you the grace to endure and even prosper through the trial. Never give up and never give into the temptations of despair from the devil. Never believe Jesus doesn't care deeply for you. Someday it will all make sense. Cling to hope in your darkest hour or until your dying breath.

GOD STILL DOES MIRACLES

God still does miracles in this generation. So what is a miracle? It is supernatural intervention of God in the affairs of man. Miracles are when God steps in and does what man cannot do. They are natural events that cannot be manipulated, executed or even explained by man. Yet they happen. There is no way I planned or executed the following miracles. At least six unexplained supernatural events, which happened over those years:

1) God suddenly gave me saliva, taste buds and an appetite again.
2) My Bible and spiritual journals survived an intense fire without burned spots or soot on the pages.
3) Instantly healing the skin disease Rosacea.
4) Providing money year after year equal to my salary the last year I worked at the bank.
5) Supplying exactly the necessary funds to cover the short fall of both medical and house insurance coverage.
6) Navigating the front six icy steps while using a walker.

Being a cancer survivor has given me special compassion and opportunity to pray for cancer patients. I have prayed for many and have seen God do great and marvelous healings. Not because of my prayers but rather because when Christians gather in faith and pray believing, God shows up. At our church Reynolda, I did some checking from the year 2000 to 2006. There were 28 reported cancer patients of who 8 died and 20 lived. This is a fantastic cure rate, with 71% of the people still with us today. One man was healed three times of the same cancer. All of those who were healed were receiving medical care, but were not relying on the medical profession to heal them. Their hope was that God would use these talented doctors to bring about their healing. Ultimately, the doctors were technicians and God Almighty was the healer.

I have found, and medical research substantiates, the reality that people with positive attitudes and those who believe and trust God are far more likely to be healed than those that just accept their fate, turn bitter and angry.

Distraction is a great solution to feeling sorry for yourself. Get involved with something even though it might take great, effort or energy. The benefit is a change of focus from lying around thinking about your many pains and problems. Get your mind on something outside yourself possibly a challenge, a hobby, mission or goal. It will do great things for your well being. I purposed not to let my feeding tube interfere with mission trips to give my testimony.

So my encouragement to you, if you are wrestling with cancer, is to stop wrestling and put your future and your trust in God and believe His Word which says, "I would above all things desire for you to prosper and be in health."[1] Cooperate with the medical staff but seek God diligently for peace that passes understanding.

I have heard people say there are no miracles today. They believe miracles stopped during the first century with the death of the last apostle. You will never convince me of that! A man with experience is never at the mercy of a man with an argument. One day I had no saliva, the next day I did. God did a restorative miracle. He is alive and well and very present in the 21st century. His miraculous power is available to you as much as it was to me. "Then Peter opened his mouth, and said, "I most certainly understand now that that God is not one to show partiality."[2] What does that mean? It means He loves you as much as He does me. He does not discriminate. He wants all men to be saved. "In the sight of God our Savior who desires all men to be saved and to come to the knowledge of truth."[3] But you might be saying "Bob, I don't know Him like you do and haven't experienced what you have shared in this book. I have never heard God speak to me. I don't have assurance that I know what will happen to me when I die. I don't feel religious or worthy, due to sin in my life now and in the past." Maybe your experience has been going to church but not having a vibrant relationship knowing Jesus as your Lord and Savior. Maybe you have never invited Him into a personal relationship. I am not talking about joining a church. I am asking you to let the greatest lover of the world come into your heart and take over your life.

That can change right now with a sincere prayer asking Jesus to come into your heart. This is extremely important, the most important commitment anyone can make in life. No one knows when our time on Earth will be over. It is so easy to say, I will think about this later. This decision will determine your eternal destiny forever.

It is written in the Bible, there is only one way to heaven, and that is through Jesus Christ.

"I am the way, the truth, and the life. No one comes to the Father but through Me. If you had known Me you would have known My Father also."

John 14:6-7

No one will enter heaven because he is a good person. "For all sinned and fall short of the glory of God."[4] But God provided a way out of our sins. "For the wages of sin is death, but the free gift of God is eternal life in Christ Jesus our Lord."[5] The good news is God still loved us even when we were unlovable. "But God commanded His love toward us, in that while we were yet sinners, Christ died for us."[6] When we recognize, confess, and repent our sinfulness, we receive God's forgiveness. "If we confess our sins, He is faithful and righteous to forgive us our sins, and to cleanse us from all unrighteousness."[7]

If you are not sure where you will spend eternity, follow me in this simple prayer. Right now. Say out loud, right where you are. That's right, right now, out loud.

Heavenly Father I know I am a sinner and I need a Savior. I know I am not worthy, but I am asking Jesus to come into my heart and take over my life. Father cleanses me of all present and past sins. Set me free! I believe Jesus that You hung on a cross and died for my sins and arose from the dead and are seated with Your Father in heaven today. You are coming back again for me. I accept the sacrifice that You made for me now. I'm born again now. I am forgiven and I am on my way to heaven because I have Jesus in my heart. I want to live for you Jesus. I want to become all you designed me to become when you created me. Give me a purpose and a destiny. Amen.

There you did it! Now go forth and tell someone what you did.

You cannot be certain of the future, but you can be certain of who controls the future! I believe as Oswald Chambers says, "The real meaning of eternal life is a life that can face anything you have to face without wavering. If you take this view, life will be become one great romance—a glorious opportunity of seeing wonderful things all the time."[D-1]

WHAT DOES THE FUTURE HOLD?

The title of this book is *Does God Really Care?* The clear evidence of the Father's caring was demonstrated by sending His only Son to earth to redeem us from our sins through the atonement on the cross so we could enjoy eternity with Him in heaven.

I hope we have shown on a much smaller scale the specific ways that God very much cares for us beyond our ability to grasp or understand. He showed us over and over again His love from the smallest details of finding a certain kind of curtain rod to magnificent miracles. Things that were important to us in fixing up the house He wonderfully supplied. He cares. He cares very deeply about His children just as you care very deeply about your children. Little important things to them become important to you. Your heavenly Father is far more loving and caring than any of us could ever hope to be. Please believe God really cares for you!

As we come to the end of this book it is important to understand its purposes. This book was not meant to be a work of fiction, bibliography, prophetic, theological or even particularly biblical. It is a living testimony, our testimony. There are four purposes in writing this book. The primary reason is to be a legacy to our children and grandchildren. The second is to simply tell what Jesus has done for us through difficult times. The third is to help others going through difficulties. The last purpose was that others might gain wisdom by learning the lessons we learned walking through the past eight years.

We stand in awe and amazement of the great and mighty deeds God did for our family. We will tell of these wonders the rest of our lives. We are amazed by God's outrageous blessings during those difficult days. We look back and see the marvelous work God has done in both Gloria and me. We are not the same people today as we were then. Yes, we are older and grayer, but the real change has come from inside. Our priorities have been shuffled. We realize how the trials have drawn us closer together as a family and especially as husband and wife. It has created in both of us a desire for greater intimacy with our God that we might know Him and be fully aligned with all His purposes and plans for the remainder of our lives.

We now recognize every trial He allowed to happen as a platform on which He was revealing Himself. He was constantly showing His love and power to both of us and to others. These experiences will enable us to move into the future with wide eyed realization. He controls the future and will always be with us even as we move into the latter years of our life. Yes, right through our deaths and all through eternity.

Our hope is He will use this testimony to His Glory. It has opened a glimpse into the deep mercy and compassion of our God. I (Bob) now look upon suffering people differently. It has allowed me to understand in some small way His compassion for those who are suffering. When I see people devastated by loss through a fire, people traveling through cancer, and every time I hear a fire truck I try to remember to pray. When walking through a hospital and seeing people in pain or hearing of people in severe pain, I pray and empathize deeply. Every time I get a request from someone for a testimony tape of my healing, I lift him or her up in sustained prayer. Would I have done this before? No, I am sure that would not have been the case. We have numerous opportunities to pray for others going through trials. We are able to pray with greater faith because of what God has done for us.

There is an old Army recruiting ad that read: "Be all that you can be." The more accurate statement should read: "Be all that He wants you to be."

When I was young I worked, dreamed and strived for success in my life. I believe to some degree I achieved success by the world standards. Somewhere along the way I realized, that I was not going to be famous, renowned or rich. I gradually changed from the goal of being a big-time success to one of significance or influence. Before I leave this world, I wanted to impact the lives of others in a meaningful and lasting way. To some extent I believe I have. Now, in the latter days of my life I have evolved once again and have left success and significance behind. My goal now is to be focused only on, "I might know Him,"[1] and what He wants me to be. This does not have any specific title except His child, friend, ambassador and lover.

My experience over these years has led me to two desires of my heart. The first one is expressed in the book of Psalms. "One thing I have asked from the Lord, that I shall seek. That I may dwell in the house of the Lord all the days of my life, to behold the beauty of the Lord and to meditate in His temple."[2] My pursuit for the remaining days of my life is that I might know Him. That I might know Jesus' emotions, passions, desires, thoughts and zeal for mankind. All of which is the beauty of the Lord. My hope is for fresh revelation to know Him in a more intimate way, to know His actions on earth and His movements among men.

My second desire is in the book of Revelation, that I might prepare myself for the next season of my life. I realize this life is a mere test, for most of us a scant 70, 80, 90 years of preparation. A dress rehearsal for my real life in the age to come which is the millennium followed by eternity. What I do during this life will determine the role, responsibility, dominion, power and personal relationship I will have with Jesus forever and ever. My goal is revealed in the book of Revelation. "To have garments of white linen, which are the righteous acts of saints."[3] My understanding of the righteous acts of the saints is simply being a blessing to people. Always looking for ways I can bless the people that God brings into my life. My focus from this point is set. The purpose of my life belongs to God, not me.

I now understand my main purpose of why I am on this earth. It is to bring glory to God! I didn't understand when I was younger. I thought it was to bring glory to me. Now my purpose is clear, my goal is established, my course set for the rest of my days.

So how do I do that in a practical way? I give glory to God many different ways. One way is I minister to my wife, kids, and grandchildren by being available and willing to do things for them I don't necessarily want to do. I minister to God by giving Him glory in my financial giving, prayer time, praying for others, being an effective leader. God also receives glory by my having a right response to my neighbors, friends and those that reject me. I give Him glory through joy, peace, and contentment and yes even in pain and suffering. There are other ways but I will be content if I can be faithful to these.

So what are my final thoughts over these past years? My hope and prayer is my entire family will follow in our footsteps. Gloria and I have no idea what the future holds, but we are convinced the past eight years will help us face the future victoriously. As the ever-expanding number of our grandchildren grows, it is our prayer this testimony will be passed down through the generations. That this true story will be passed along to the entire Robert C. Bruce clan for all to know the great and mighty deeds of our God in the early years of the 21st century. We hope it will a blessing and encouragement to many who are going through trials and tribulations.

Authors Note:

Thank you so much for taking your time to read our testimony. If you would like for me to give this testimony to your church or group please contact me. If you would like to order additional copies of this book please contact me.

Bob Bruce
4050 Winchester Rd.
Winston-Salem NC 27106

Phone: 336-773-1211
E-Mail bgbruce@triad.rr.com

SCRIPTURES

Chapter 3: Tell the Great Deeds God Has Done
1. Matthew 6:25*
2. Ephesians 6:13

Chapter 4: Our Family Grows
1. Proverbs 19:14
2. Psalm 127:3
3. Psalm 127:5

Chapter 8: Rebuilding Adventure
1. Philippians 4:19
2. Proverbs 23:7
3. Proverbs 15:15

Chapter 9: Discouragement
1. Psalm 119:50
2. Psalm 50:15
3. Romans 8:37
4. 2Corinthians 12:9
5. Psalm 27:13
6. Psalm 40:2
7. 1 Peter1: 6-7
8. Romans 8:18
9. Job 1: 13-19, Job 2:7-9

Chapter 10: Wilderness Experience
1. Song of Solomon 2:9
2. Deuteronomy 31:6
3. Ecclesiastes 3:11

Chapter 11: Favor of the Lord
1. Isaiah 55:8-9
2. Daniel 3:27
3. Proverbs 3:24
4. Psalm 86:15
5. Philippians 4:19
6. Psalm 127:1

Chapter 12: Wisdom Gained
1. Romans 8:28
2. Job 5:17
3. 1Peter 4:12
4. Psalm 18:29
5. John 10:10
6. Ephesians 3:20
7. Luke 22:32
8. Hebrews 11:6
9. Jeremiah 29:11

Chapter 13: Your Own Trials
1. John 16:33
2. Romans 3:5
3. Psalm 46:1
4. 1Corinthians 10:13
5. Psalm 34:17

Chapter 14: God Still Does Miracles
1. 3 John 1:2
2. Acts 10:34
3. 1Timothy 2:4
4. Romans 3:23
5. Romans 5:8

6. Romans 6:23
7. 1 John 1:9

Chapter 15: What Does the Future Hold?
1. Philippians 3:10
2. Psalm 27:4
3. Revelation 19:7

All scriptures are from the New American Standard Bible

NOTES

A-1 Corrie Ten Boom, *The Hiding Place,* written by John Sherrill published by Guidepost in 1971.

B-1 Robert C. Bruce, *Executive Job Search Strategies, The Guide for* Career Transitions, 1994 by VGM Career Horizons, A division of NTC Publishing in Lincolnwood, Illinois USA

C-1 James Fillmore, from *I Am Resolved,* the living Hymns, pg. 571.

D-1 Glenn A Pearson, *Prepare to Meet your God: Scriptural Meditations* for the Terminally Ill & Their *Caregivers* published in 2006 by Genesis Press Lincoln, Nebraska USA.

E-1Oswald Chambers *My Utmost for His Highest,* published in 1992 by Oswald Chambers Publications Association, Ltd Grand Rapids, MI

Printed in the United States
113027LV00002B/301-999/P